Music, Love and
103

Love Me Please

Also available from NBM Comics Biographies:
The Beatles in Comics
The Rolling Stones in Comics
Bob Marley in Comics
Michael Jackson in Comics
The Disney Bros.
Elvis
Einstein

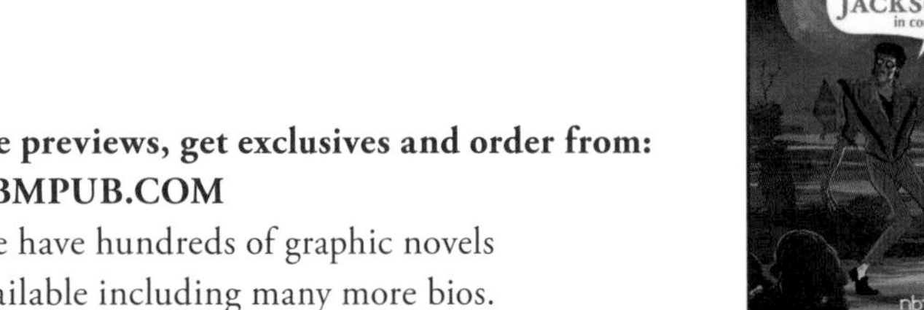

See previews, get exclusives and order from:
NBMPUB.COM
We have hundreds of graphic novels
available including many more bios.
Subscribe to our monthly newsletter
Follow us on Facebook & Instagram
(nbmgraphicnovels), Twitter (@nbmpub).

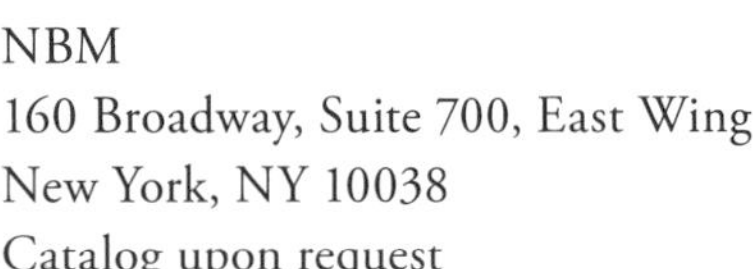

NBM
160 Broadway, Suite 700, East Wing
New York, NY 10038
Catalog upon request

ISBN 9781681122762

Library of Congress Control Number: 2021937285
Translation by Montana Kane
Lettering by Ortho
Printed in China
1st printing August 2021

This book is also available wherever e-books are sold, ISBN 9781681122779

GRAPHIC NOVELS
Comics Biographies

Writer **NICOLAS FINET** * Art **CHRISTOPHER** * Color **DEGREFF**

THE STORY OF JANIS JOPLIN (1943-1970)

PREFACE

by Gilbert Shelton

Janis died fifty years ago! Gosh! She and I were good friends ever since we were students together at the University of Texas in 1962 or '63. She would be in her late 70's by now... hard to imagine. What a great, cranky old lady she would have made.

I have already related my best Janis stories elsewhere, and I don't want to repeat myself. The last time I saw Janis was in San Francisco in the summer of 1968. She took me for a ride in her Porsche Speedster convertible which had been painted with psychedelic images by a fan.

Christopher's biography of Janis doesn't deal with her legend, only with the facts. Christopher's clean and simple drawing style is ideal for this subject. I learned a lot about Janis that I didn't know before.

Gilbert Shelton

Thanks to Élisabeth Bailly, Jean-Michel Dupont, Sophie Chédru, Hélène Gédouin and the Marabulles team. Special thanks to Madeleine De-Mille for allowing us to make a friendly nod to the character of Ray Banana, in tribute to Ted Benoit, and of course to Gilbert Shelton, in the good care of Férid Keddour / Thé-Troc and Lora Fountain, for his warm preface. Jean-Paul Pécréaux, Patrick Montier for their help and documentation: it's starting to become a habit.

BESSIE SMITH
ODETTA
MA RAINEY
You were just a tiny little thing, the first time we heard you...
AMERICAN
TEXACO

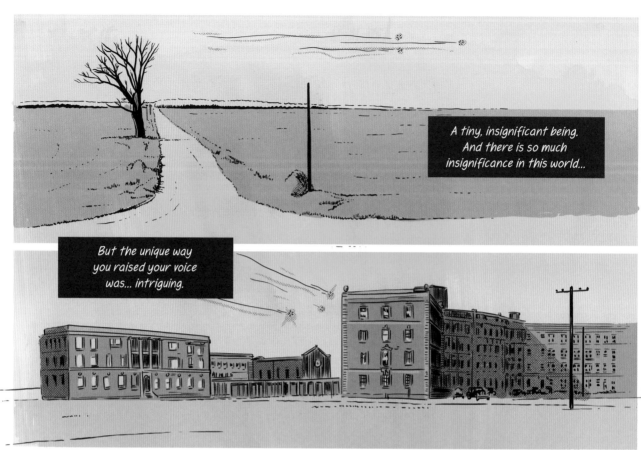

A tiny, insignificant being.
And there is so much
insignificance in this world...

But the unique way
you raised your voice
was... intriguing.

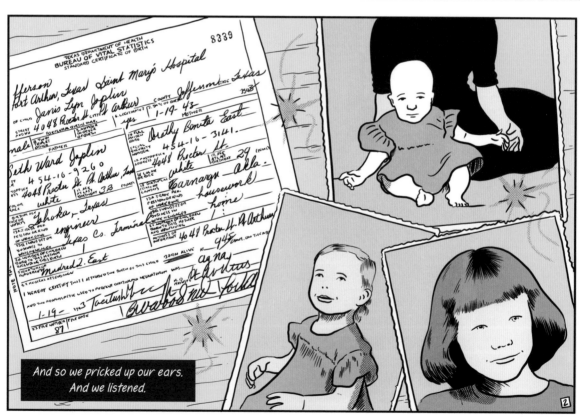

And so we pricked up our ears.
And we listened.

CHAPTER 1

Forget Port Arthur

BUT WHY, DADDY?
WHY ARE THEY TAKING OUR PIANO?

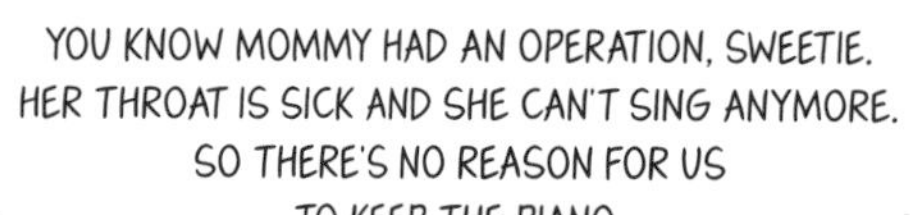
YOU KNOW MOMMY HAD AN OPERATION, SWEETIE. HER THROAT IS SICK AND SHE CAN'T SING ANYMORE. SO THERE'S NO REASON FOR US TO KEEP THE PIANO.

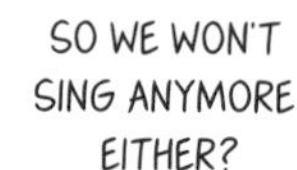
SO WE WON'T SING ANYMORE EITHER?

SURE WE WILL, PUMPKIN.
WE'LL SING.

JUST... DIFFERENTLY.
4

BACK SO SOON, KIDDO?
You were drawn to the arts early on. To images, first.
1955

AND YOU'RE DRAWING AGAIN... WHAT A SURPRISE.

EXACTLY! AND YOU KNOW WHAT, DAD? THE SCHOOL PAPER, THE DRIFTWOOD, IS GOING TO PUBLISH SOME OF MY DRAWINGS IN THE NEXT ISSUE!

MY ART TEACHER EVEN TOLD ME THERE'S A COFFEE SHOP THAT WANTS TO PUT UP SOME OF MY--
JANIS !

WHAT'S WITH YOUR MOTHER?
JANIS !
ARE YOU TWO ARGUING AGAIN?
5

JANIS! WHAT THE HECK IS THIS?
BUT MOM...
IT'S JUST A DRAWING, THAT'S ALL.

THIS... THIS HORROR?
JUST A DRAWING?

WHAT, MOM?

WHAT'S THE PROBLEM?

YOU KNOW EXACTLY WHAT IT IS! GET THAT IMAGE OF DEBAUCHERY OUT OF THE HOUSE. NOW!
6

"Summertime" by George Gershwin, DuBose Heyward, © 1935.

Summertime
HEBERT
85 W 416
WHAT A VOICE, MY FRIENDS, WHAT A VOICE! THAT WAS "SUMMERTIME" ON KFDM, THE UNFORGETTABLE VERSION SUNG BY BILLIE HOLIDAY. AND WHAT A BEAUTIFUL WAY TO CONTINUE THIS GORGEOUS DAY OF DECEMBER 1955 IN PORT ARTHUR...
ALL RIGHT, GIRLS, EVERYTHING LOOKS OKAY HERE.
SORRY, MRS. HEBERT, BUT WHEN I REALLY GET INTO A SONG...
...I TEND TO FORGET WHERE I AM!
WHICH TENDS TO GET ON MY FAMILY'S NERVES.
NO DEED TO APOLOGIZE, JANIS! WE'LL NEVER CRITICIZE YOU FOR SINGING IN THIS PLACE. BESIDES, I'M SURE YOU'VE BEEN TOLD THIS BEFORE, BUT I FIND YOU HAVE A VERY... ENGAGING VOICE.
8

You wanted to try the theater, too.
DAVE, WHAT ARE WE DOING FOR THE SET OF SCENE 2?
HOW SHOULD I KNOW? GO ASK THE NEW GIRL, THERE.
ORT ARTHUR LITTLE THEATER
SEASON 1957
HI THERE. JANE, RIGHT?
JANIS.
I HEARD YOU HAVE A GIFT FOR DESIGNING AND PAINTING SETS, JANIS. AND RIGHT NOW, WE NEED AN IDEA FOR THE DANCING SCENE ON THE PLAZA.
REALLY? SOMEONE SAID I WAS GIFTED? COOL. I'LL GIVE IT MY BEST SHOT, THEN.
ALL RIGHT, THAT'S ENOUGH FOR TODAY, GUYS. I'M OUT OF HERE. ANYONE COMING?
WHERE?
TO SABINE LAKE, AS ALWAYS.
WHAT'S AT THE LAKE?
9

IT'S CALLED ON THE ROAD, AND THE AUTHOR'S NAME IS JACK KEROUAC. IT'S HUGE, MAN! HUGE!
HMM. UNFORTUNATELY, THERE'S NO WAY MY PARENTS WOULD HAVE A BOOK LIKE THAT AT HOME.
SOUTHERN COMFORT
TO THINK LOUISIANA IS JUST ON THE OTHER SIDE OF THE LAKE... I HEAR IT'S GREAT, OVER THERE!
HEY, JIM LANGDON, WHEN ARE YOU TAKING ME TO NEW ORLEANS? LET'S GO! CAN WE?
TAKE SOME LITTLE BRAT TO GO PARTY ACROSS THE LAKE? YEAH, RIGHT!
WHAT??!
WHAT DID YOU CALL ME, YOU MOTHERFUCKER?
HA! HA! HA!
HA! HA!
YOU KNOW WHAT THE BRAT SAYS?!
10

HA! HA! HA!
LANGDON, YOU *HAVE* TO TAKE ME TO LOUISIANA! THAT'S AN ORDER, MAN!
HA!
HA!
OK, OK... YOU WIN, JANIS.

D'YOU SEE THE NEW *MAD*? KURTZMAN, MAN. THE GUY'S A GODDAMNED GENIUS!
COME ON. PEACE, BABE. I PROMISE TO TAKE YOU ACROSS THE LAKE.

YOU KNOW HOW TO TALK TO LADIES, ASSHOLE.

*Used here ironically to make fun of the way Texans referred to black people at the time.

"Empty Bed Blues" by Bessie Smith, © 1928.

CHECK OUT THE CRAZY CHICK... D'YOU SEE HOW SHE STRUTS?
HEY, HONEY, WOW. YOUR SEX APPEAL'S GOT MY HANES ON FIRE.
ALL RIGHT, YOUNG PEOPLE, SETTLE DOWN AND BE QUIET, PLEASE!
GENTLEMEN...
MMH. SORRY: *LADY* AND GENTLEMEN.
YOU ARE INDEED A MINORITY HERE, YOUNG LADY. IF I'M NOT MISTAKEN, YOU ARE THE ONLY MEMBER OF THE WEAKER SEX HERE AT THE START OF THE 1958 SCHOOL YEAR.
WEAKER? THAT REMAINS TO BE SEEN.
AND HOW DO YOU INTEND TO STAND OUT THIS YEAR, MISS... MMH... JOPLIN? BY BEING INSOLENT?
IF I WERE YOU, I WOULDN'T PLAY THAT... MMH... RISKY GAME... THAT AND YOUR... MMH... ECCENTRIC ATTIRE COULD BE SETBACKS.
D'YOU HEAR THE WAY HE TALKED TO YOU? AND HE WAS BEING NICE...
IF I WERE YOU, DOLL, I'D COME TO CLASS WITH A GARBAGE CAN OVER MY HEAD. PLUS, IT WOULD MATCH YOUR LOOK.
YOU CAN'T GET OVER IT, CAN YOU? I BET YOU IRONED YOUR SUIT ALL NICE AND ALL, JUST LIKE YOUR FUDDY-DUDDY OLD MAN, RIGHT?
14

HERE'S SOME CHANGE. GO BUY YOURSELF SOMETHING PRESENTABLE, YOU STUPID BROAD!
BLING!

FUCK YOU, MAN.

THANKS FOR WAITING FOR ME. LET'S SPLIT!
THAT'S RIGHT, GO ROLL WITH YOUR DARKIES.. YUCK! THAT'S DISGUSTING!
AND ASK YOUR NEGROES TO GET YOU TO TAN A LITTLE! IT'LL FIX YOUR UGLY SKIN!

MAN, I JUST CAN'T TAKE THOSE ASSHOLES ANYMORE...
LET IT GO, JANIS. DON'T PROVOKE THEM, YOU'LL ONLY MAKE IT WORSE.

RRIIIINNG
HELLO?

HEY, FAT COW! CAN YOU STILL GET YOUR FAT ASS THROUGH THE DOOR? WHEN ARE YOU GONNA SMASH YOUR PIMPLES OFF YOUR UGLY MUG?
CLIC

15

Then there was that evening in the winter of '58, when things suddenly took on a new dimension...
DAVE, GUESS WHAT?! I CAN SING!! I CAN REALLY SING!
JANIS, RELAX... WHAT IS IT? WHAT'S GOING ON?
IT WAS LAST NIGHT... WE LEFT PASEA'S, THE COFFEE SHOP, AND HEADED FOR THE BEACH...

PASEA'S
COFFEE SHOP
PASEA'S COFFEE SHOP
THAT WAS COOL OF PASEA TO LET YOU PUT UP YOUR DRAWINGS, JANIS.
YEAH. GOOD THING WE HAVE THE COFFEE SHOP... WITHOUT IT, NUTHIN'!
WHERE TO, GUYS? THE BEACH?

THE BEACH IT IS!

LET'S HAVE SOME TUNES!
WOOHOO!
SOUTHERN COMFORT
16

"Love Me Tender" by George R. Poulton.Vera Matson, Elvis Presley © 1956. "Alabama Bound", Robert Hoffman, © 1909.

And as if that weren't enough, shortly afterwards, you finally went where you had dreamed of going, sweetheart...
PRESERVATION

BOURBON STREET! THE FRENCH QUARTER! AND WE CAN PARTY ALL GODDAMN NIGHT! WOOHOOOOO!

I CAN'T BELIEVE WE'RE HERE, GUYS!! THIS IS AWESOME! WE'RE FINALLY IN NEW ORLEANS!!

AND YOU'RE DRUNK, TO BOOT! DO YOU REALIZE HOW MUCH TROUBLE, YOU'RE IN, YOUNG LADY? YOU'RE A MINOR! ONE OF MY COLLEAGUES IS CALLING YOUR PARENTS. WE'LL SEE WHAT THEY SAY.

I'M REALLY SORRY, SIR... IT WAS RAINING REALLY HARD, AND THE CAR SKIDDED AND I LOST CONTROL...

PETE, DO YOU COPY?

18

PETE HERE. I COPY.
WE GOT THE GIRL'S PARENTS ON THE HORN. THEY'RE FURIOUS. THEY DID GIVE HER PERMISSION TO USE THE CAR, BUT NOT TO GO GET LIQUORED UP IN LOUISIANA!
WHAT ABOUT THE OTHERS?
THE PARENTS VOUCH FOR THEM. SAY NONE OF THE BOYS ARE DANGEROUS. JUST NUTS!
YOU GOT LUCKY, BOYS. SEEING AS THE GIRL'S A MINOR, I COULD HAVE BOOKED YOU ON THE SPOT. IT'S AS SERIOUS AS A RAPE CHARGE, YOU KNOW. BUT THE YOUNG LADY'S PARENTS VOUCHED FOR YOU.

YOU'RE GETTING OFF WITH JUST THE TOW FEES AND THE REPAIR COSTS. AND A LITTLE HITCHHIKING BACK TO TEXAS! I WON'T KEEP YOU ANY LONGER.

I DON'T BELIEVE THIS, MAN! SHE BADGERS US TO GO, AND WE GET STUCK WITH THE BILL!

AS FOR YOU, MISS, I AM UNDER STRICT ORDERS TO PUT YOU ON A BUS TO PORT ARTHUR RIGHT AWAY. YOUR PARENTS WIRED THE MONEY. YOU ASK ME, YOU'RE GETTING OFF EASY.

NOW GO, AND LET THIS BE A LESSON TO YOU. I'M GUESSING YOU'RE IN FOR ONE HECK OF A SCOLDING WHEN YOU GET HOME.
TRAILWAYS
19

THIS CAN'T GO ON LIKE THIS, JANIS!
ALL THIS TROUBLEMAKING HAS EARNED YOU A NASTY REPUTATION IN TOWN! YOU JUST TURNED 18. IT'S TIME TO ACT LIKE AN ADULT!
MY REPUTATION IN TOWN? YOU THINK I CARE ABOUT WHAT THIS TOWN OF RACISTS AND MORONS THINKS OF ME?
JANIS !
LISTEN, JANIS, YOUR MOTHER AND I CAME UP WITH A TRANSITIONAL SOLUTION... SINCE YOU STUDIED COMPUTER PUNCH CARDS AND SINCE A LOT OF COMPANIES ARE RECRUITING IN THAT FIELD, ESPECIALLY OUT WEST...
...WE FEEL THAT GETTING AWAY FROM HERE FOR A BIT WOULD BE GOOD FOR YOU. YOUR AUNTS BARBARA AND MIMI, IN L.A., HAVE AGREED TO TAKE YOU IN FOR A WHILE.
COMPUTER PUNCH CARD OPERATOR... *SIGH* NOT EXACTLY MY DREAM, EVEN IF IT IS ON THE COAST. YOU KNOW ALL I REALLY WANT IS TO BE AN ARTIST!
I'M REALLY WORRIED ABOUT HER, SETH...
DON'T TORTURE YOURSELF. A DRASTIC CHANGE OF ENVIRONMENT WILL OPEN UP NEW OPPORTUNITIES FOR HER.
BUT SHE IS SO UNBELIEVABLY STUBBORN...
20

ALL RIGHT, KIDDO... YOU'RE GOOD TO GO!
I'LL SEND NEWS REAL SOON, DAD. IT'S ALL GOING TO BE FINE.
THIS IS THE LAST CALL FOR PASSENGERS HEADED TO LOS ANGELES: PLEASE BOARD NOW!
WEST NORTH 10 70 99 os Angeles
SOUTH WEST 91 395 18 Riverside
NORTH EAST 15 91 395 18 San Bernardino

YOU'LL LIKE IT HERE.
D'YOU JUST GET INTO TOWN, YOUNG LADY?
NO. I'M FROM TEXAS BUT I LIVE HERE. I WAS LIVING WITH MY AUNTS ON LA CIENEGA, BUT I NEED PEACE AND QUIET TO PAINT. I'M AN ARTIST, SEE...

AN ARTIST? YOU SURE YOU'RE GONNA BE ABLE TO MAKE RENT?
DON'T WORRY ABOUT THE MONEY, SIR. I'VE GOT A REAL JOB, AT THE BANK OF AMERICA.
Finocchio's
SWISS CHALET
7up
100
COCKTAILS

UNTIL I MAKE IT AS AN ARTIST, OF COURSE!
I'LL TAKE THE ROOM. I LOVE THIS NEIGHBORHOOD!

And that is quite possibly the moment where it all truly started...
22

Towards the end of that summer, you even headed 400 miles north, to San Francisco...
One little escapade that was too short, but enough for you to know you would be going back there. Soon.
23

THIS BANK IS YOUR BANK, THIS BANK IS MY BANK !

HELLO PEOPLE, THIS IS BENNY HOROWITZ, BACK AFTER THE COMMERCIAL BREAK, TALKING TO YOU FROM THE KFDM STUDIO IN BEAUMONT, TEXAS!

GOD BLESS THIS NEW BEAUTIFUL YEAR 1962, MY FRIENDS!

HAVE YOU SEEN MY OUTFIT?

STAFF ONLY

LANGDON, I CAN'T TAKE THIS CRAP ANYMORE...

AND I'VE ONLY BEEN BACK FROM CALIFORNIA THREE WEEKS!

JANIS... TRY LOOKING AT THE POSITIVE SIDE. YOU MAKE A LITTLE DOUGH AND YOU HAVE A CERTAIN AMOUNT OF FREEDOM.

THAT'S GOING A LITTLE FAR, JANIS. THERE'S COOL STUFF HERE. LIKE WHEN THEY LET US DO A FEW NUMBERS AT THE PURPLE ONION IN HOUSTON. DON'T TELL ME YOU DON'T LIKE THAT. AND WHEN WE GO PARTYING IN LOUISIANA OR AUSTIN...
COME ON, MAN, TAKE IT EASY. WE'LL RELAX OVER DRINKS TONIGHT AT BUSTER'S, OKAY?

The BUSTER'S

FEELING BETTER? DON'T TELL ME YOU DON'T GET A KICK OUT OF THE VIBE IN HERE!

OF COURSE I DIG IT, BUT IT'S THE MENTALITY, JIM. EVERYONE HERE IS SO... CONVENTIONAL, AND SQUARE! IT DRIVES ME NUTS!

YOU KNOW, LANGDON, I THOUGHT ABOUT WHAT YOU SAID EARLIER... AND WHERE WE COULD TRY SOMETHING NEW...

AUSTIN.
The BUSTER'S
25

YOU REALLY NEED TO MAKE AN EFFORT, JANIS.
DON'T WORRY, MOM. I LIKE THIS SCHOOL AND AUSTIN SEEMS GREAT.
WELL IF IT'S ALL AS NICE AS THIS CAFETERIA, THEN...
YOU CAN GO HOME WITH PEACE OF MIND, MOM.
YOUR FATHER AND I ARE COUNTING ON YOU, HONEY.
DON'T LET US DOWN.

DID YOU JUST START HERE AT UT?* NOT ALWAYS EASY, IS IT?
SIGH TELL ME ABOUT IT. WHAT'S THE SECRET TO THE BEST PARTIES AND STUFF ON CAMPUS?

UM, I DUNNO... KEEP YOUR EYES AND EARS OPEN. HANG OUT. AND READ THIS, TOO.
IT'S THE BEST STUDENT PAPER ON CAMPUS! YOU'LL FIND WHAT YOU NEED IN THERE.
Ranger
SEPTEMBER 1962
25¢
HA HA, THIS COMIC STRIP CRACKS ME UP.
YEAH, SHELTON. THE GUY'S AMAZING!
SO WHAT'S THIS PLACE THEY MENTION IN THE ARTICLE? THE... GHETTO?
EXACTLY THE PLACE YOU'RE LOOKING FOR, DOLL!
26

*University of Texas at Austin, often abbreviated as UT.

DRUGS
Walgreen
Enjoy Austin Maid ICE CREAM
SAVE in the MUTUAL SAVING INSTITUTION
CUSTOMER PARKING
HEY, HI. I'M, UM... LOOKING FOR A PLACE CALLED... THE GHETTO, OR SOMETHING. DOES THAT RING A BELL?
RELAX, LITTLE SISTER. AND WELCOME TO THE GHETTO. NOBODY GETS TURNED DOWN HERE.
ANYONE WHO NEEDS A BREAK, NEEDS TO DODGE THE FUZZ, OR JUST NEEDS A MATTRESS FOR THE NIGHT, WE FIND THEM SOME ROOM.
HERE, HAVE A DRINK. WHAT'S YOUR NAME?
27

FRIENDS... SOME OF YOU ALREADY KNOW HER FROM CAMPUS... JANIS JOPLIN!

What Good can drinkin' do ...ooo

Lord, I drink all night but the next day I still feel blue

There's a glass on the table, they say it's gonna ease my pain

But I drink it down, an' the next day I feel the same

Gimme whiskey gimme bourbon gimme gin

Cause it don't matter what I drinkin', Lord, as long as it drown this sorrow I'm in

You wowed them from the get-go, sweetheart.

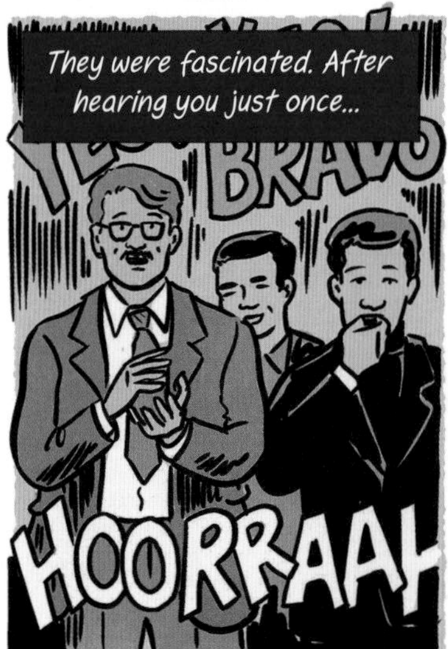

They were fascinated. After hearing you just once...
BRAVO
HOORRAAH

THANK YOU, THANK YOU! YOU GUYS ARE GREAT!
28

"What Good Can Drinkin' Do" by Janis Joplin. © 1962

...they couldn't
get enough of you.

I'M HERE, GUYS.
LET'S HIT THE GHETTO!

WHAT THE HELL ARE YOU
DOING? YOU COMIN'
OR WHAT?
29

HOLY CRAP, JACK... THAT BLEW MY MIND. IT WAS AMAZING!
LA DOLCE VITA
BORDER'S

THOSE EUROPEANS ARE AT A WHOLE DIFFERENT LEVEL... IF ONLY WE COULD DO THAT HERE...

TRUE, THEY HAVE SOMETHING WE DON'T. LOOK AT THEIR MUSIC SCENE, WITH THAT NEW BAND THAT'S GOT LONDON TALKING. THE ROLLING STONES.
BUT THAT'S MORE ROCK, RIGHT?
HEY, JANIS!

HI, GORGEOUS! CORRUPTING YOUNG MEN, I SEE...

JULIE! OH MY GOD, I LOVE YOUR CAR!

WELL THEN HOP IN, LET'S GO FOR A RIDE!

ARE YOU JANIS?
OUCH, YOU DON'T LOOK TOO GOOD...

I'M SICK OF THIS SHIT. ME AND JULIE GOT INTO ANOTHER BIG FIGHT.
It brings a tear into my eyes
When I begin to
realize I've cried
so much since you've
been gone

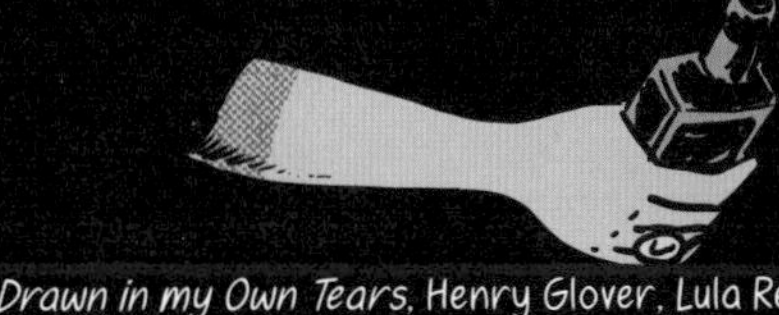

Drawn in my Own Tears, Henry Glover, Lula Reed, © 1951

You became a local celebrity in under two months.
SHE LOOKS WEIRD, BUT DAMN CAN THAT BROAD SING!
NO KIDDING! I HEAR THEY GAVE HER A REGULAR SLOT ON WEDNESDAYS AT THE CHUCK WAGON.
LEADBELLY, PETE SEEGER, ROSIE MADDOX... HER REPERTOIRE IS TOP-NOTCH!
WELL I FOR ONE AM GOING BACK TO SEE HER NEXT WEEK!

Everybody was drawn to your spontaneity and generosity...
HEY JANIS, YOU'RE FAMOUS! CHECK OUT THE BLURB IN THE SUMMER TEXAN...

They just needed to appreciate your... uniqueness.
NOW THAT'S A COMPLIMENT...
SHE GOES BAREFOOT IF SHE FEES LIKE IT, SHE DARES TO BE DIFFERENT. HER NAME IS JANIS JOPLIN... YOWZA!

SHE OFTEN SINGS LEAD VOCALS IN A LOCAL BAND CALLED THE WALLER CREEK BOYS, WHOSE TWO OTHER MEMBERS ARE POWELL ST. JOHN AND LANNY WIGGINS...

HOW'S THAT FEEL, BOYS? SHE'S HERE FIVE MINUTES AND SHE NABS THE LIMELIGHT! HAPPY?
32

CUT IT OUT, LARRY. WE ALL LIVE AT THE GHETTO. CAN YOU IMAGINE IF WE DIDN'T GET ALONG? WE'RE ALL IN THIS TOGETHER.

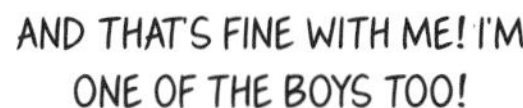
AND THAT'S FINE WITH ME! I'M ONE OF THE BOYS TOO!

But UT, in part because of your drinking and your excess, quickly seemed boring to you. You needed more... intensity.
THAT WOULD BE FANTASTIC, MR. THREADGILL! AND A GREAT HONOR FOR US!
AND YOU COULD PLAY EVERY WEDNESDAY, LIKE AT THE CHUCK WAGON.

THINK ABOUT IT, YOUNG PEOPLE.
IF YOU COMMIT TO ME, IT'S A SERIOUS THING.

I CAN CALL YOU KENNETH, RIGHT?
YOU HAVE OUR WORD, KENNETH!
THREADGILL'S

Walk Right In, Gus Cannon, Hosea Woods © 1929

UNIVERSITY NEWS

5¢

AUSTIN, TEXAS

MONDAY DECEMBER 9, 1962

PRICE 5 CENTS

JANIS WINS UGLIEST MAN!!

Alpha Phi Omega

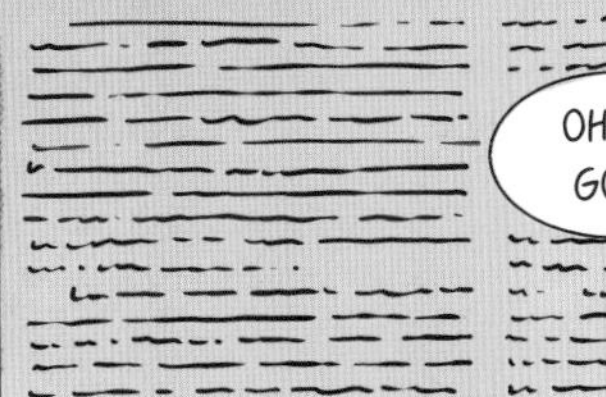

D'YOU HEAR ABOUT JANIS?
YUP.
WHO WROTE THAT CRAP, ANYWAY?
REMEMBER THOSE JERKS SHE MOCKED IN PUBLIC AT THREADGILL'S THE OTHER NIGHT? LOOK NO FURTHER.
AND THE WORST PART IS, THOSE MORONS AT THE DAILY TEXAN PICKED UP THE STORY. THEY THOUGHT IT WAS FUNNY.
OUCH.
OUCH IS RIGHT.
WHERE IS SHE?
IN THE BACK, WITH POWELL AND CHET.
CHET?
CHET HELMS. USED TO BE A STUDENT AT UT, KNOWS EVERYONE IN FRISCO. HE'S ALREADY TOURED QUITE A BIT AND STOPS BY HERE ON A REGULAR BASIS.
LET'S LEAVE HER ALONE. THIS ISN'T THE RIGHT TIME.
36

YOU SURE YOU WANT TO LEAVE, JANIS?
YEP! I DON'T CARE ABOUT COLLEGE OR A DEGREE. THEY DON'T LIKE ME? WELL THE FEELING IS MUTUAL!
COOKING
THREADGILL'S
6416 N. LAMAR
Threadgill's Exit
BUT WHAT ABOUT YOUR FAMILY?
LISTEN, I TURN 20 IN A FEW DAYS. I'M BIG ENOUGH TO MAKE MY OWN DECISIONS. I WROTE MY PARENTS A LETTER. I THINK THEY'LL UNDERSTAND.
BESIDES... I WANT TO LIVE IN THE MIDDLE OF THAT CREATIVE VIBE I FELT ALL OVER CALIFORNIA. IF I DON'T DO IT NOW, MAN, I'LL ALWAYS REGRET IT.
OK, IF THAT'S WHAT YOU WANT...
THIS IS IT, THEN! SAN FRANCISCO, HERE WE COME!
HOME
37

DOG N SUDS
CHAR-CO BURGERS
ROOT BEER
THE LIMIT DRIVE IN COLD DRINKS
ROOT BEER
I HOPE MY FAMILY WON'T BE TOO...
TOO WHAT?
TOO MUCH OF A PAIN.
HEY, MOM.
YOU DIDN'T TELL ME YOU'D BE BRINGING A YOUNG WOMAN WITH YOU.
GOOD GOD, LOOK AT YOURSELVES! YOU LOOK LIKE VAGRANTS!
HEY, HOW ABOUT A BEER?
?!
38

LORD, BLESS THIS HUMBLE MEAL AND FILL OUR STARVING SOULS! AND MAY YOUR INFINITE GOODNESS EXTEND TO MY SON CHESTER, WHO IS ON THE ROAD TO PERDITION... AMEN!
SO, WHERE ARE YOU SPENDING THE NIGHT?
ER... WE THOUGHT WE'D STAY HERE.
GOOD LORD, WITH *THAT* GIRL?! UNDER MY ROOF?
BUT MOM, WE'RE NOT LOVERS, WE'RE JUST FRIENDS.
IT'S OUT OF THE QUESTION, DO YOU HEAR ME?! NOT ON YOUR LIFE! END OF DISCUSSION!
I'M REALLY SORRY, BRO. BUT YOU KNOW HOW CLOSED-MINDED SHE CAN BE.
I KNOW, DON'T WORRY. AND THANKS FOR THE RIDE.
HERE WE GO, HONEY. BACK ON THE ROAD.
TIME AND TIME AGAIN.
39

FRISCO! NORTH BEACH! WE FINALLY MADE IT! CAN YOU FREAKING BELIEVE IT, CHET?! JUST LIKE KEROUAC, GINSBERG AND THE OTHERS... NOW IT'S OUR TURN!

YEP. COME ON, LET'S GET CLEANED UP. MY BUDDY DAVE FREIBERG IS EXPECTING US.

DAMN THAT SHOWER FELT GOOD, AFTER 50 HOURS ON THE ROAD!
YEAH, YOU GUYS WEREN'T A PRETTY SIGHT... OR SMELL...
DAVE'S GOT GOOD NEWS FOR YOU, JANIS.

I GOT YOU A GIG AT COFFEE AND CONFUSION, IF YOU WANT IT. IT DOESN'T PAY, BUT IT'S A GREAT PLACE TO GET EXPOSURE.
AND IT'S TONIGHT.

SERIOUSLY? TONIGHT?? SHIT, THAT'S... I MEAN... YEAH, GREAT.
SURE. THAT'D BE NEAT.
40

Stealin' Stealin', The Memphis Jug Band, © around 1925

EAAHH! COOL! WOO!!
RIGHT ON!!
BRAVO!!

MY DARLINGS, YOU KNOW THAT WE DON'T PLAY FOR MONEY HERE, BUT THE KID WAS SO AMAZING THAT I THINK WE SHOULD MAKE AN EXCEPTION TONIGHT! WE'RE GOING TO PASS AROUND THE HAT. GIVE FROM THE HEART! FOR JANIS!!

And that's how it finally started to happen. How it all really started.

YOU REALLY HIT THE JACKPOT, DOLL... 50 BUCKS! CAN YOU BELIEVE IT?

A LOT OF CATS DON'T EVEN MAKE THAT MUCH AFTER SEVERAL MONTHS!

I TOLD YOU YOU'D BLOW PEOPLE'S MINDS IN SAN FRANCISCO!

CHAPTER 2

The Temptation of Disaster

CITY LIGHTS BOOKS
BOOKS
CITY LIGHTS BOOKS
BOOKS

600 ASHBURY
HAIGHT
The UNIQUE MEN'S Shop

44

THIS IS IT. THIS IS GONNA BE OUR CRIB FOR A WHILE.
WOW, MAN! IT LOOKS GREAT!

WELL, *GREAT*, I DUNNO... WAIT TILL YOU SEE INSIDE.

HEY, CHET.
HEY, RODNEY. THIS IS JANIS, A FRIEND.

RODNEY'S UNCLE OWNS THIS HOUSE: 22 ROOMS THAT HE RENTS OUT TO STUDENTS, ARTISTS, AND BEATNIKS PASSING THROUGH.

NOT TO MENTION A FEW, WELL-INTENTIONED DR. FEELGOOD'S!
AND THIS IS RODNEY. HE'S LIKE THE PRISON WARDEN.

LET'S SEE, WHERE SHOULD WE PUT YOU?

THIS ONE'S ALREADY FULL...
DID YOU KNOW JANIS JUST CAME IN FROM TEXAS TO START HER MUSICAL CAREER? I'M TELLING YOU, SHE'S GOING TO BLOW UP!

NO ROOM IN HERE, EITHER.
MUSIC, HUH? YOU'LL HAVE TO MEET MY BROTHER, PETER ALBIN. HE'S AROUND HERE SOMEWHERE. HE SINGS AND PLAYS BASS.

AH, NOW *HERE*, THOUGH...

YOU GUYS ARE GOING TO LIVE LIKE ROYALTY! CHECK OUT THE PALACE, JANIS!
UH-HUH... YEAH... IT'S... UM... REALLY NICE.

AND SINCE YOU'RE GONNA BE A BIG STAR, I'LL EVEN MAKE YOU A DEAL, JANIS: YOU AND CHET CAN CRASH HERE FOR FREE...
BUT IN RETURN, I GET A COMP TO ALL YOUR SHOWS. DEAL?

DEAL, SWEETHEART!
46

"Black Mountain Blues" by J.C. Johnson, © 1931.

WELL, JANIS? DID YOU BLOW THEIR MINDS AGAIN, AS USUAL?

I SURE DID, HA HA! THOSE *MOTHERFUCKERS* NEVER SAW IT COMING!

SAY, LEO, I DIDN'T KNOW YOU KEPT SUCH NICE COMPANY... WHEN ARE YOU COMING BACK TO SEE ME SING, CUTIE-PIE?

ALL RIGHT, BOYS, I GOTTA SPLIT. I HAVE ANOTHER SET... AT THE DRINKIN' GOOD IN 10 GODDAMNED MINUTES!
SOUNDS LIKE IT'S GOING WELL FOR HER.
PRETTY GOOD. PEOPLE ARE TALKING ABOUT HER.

NOTHING TOO BIG YET THOUGH, MIND YOU. SHE PASSES AROUND THE HAT, THAT'S ALL. WE SAW HER AT THE FOLK THEATER, AT ST. MICHAEL'S ALLEY IN PALO ALTO, AT THE SHELTER, IN SANTA CRUZ, ON KPFA...

...AND WITH THE GIRLS FROM ANXIOUS ASP. I HEAR SHE LIKES TO SWING BOTH WAYS, IF YOU KNOW WHAT I MEAN.
JUST FOR KICKS.
48

YOU THINK SHE HAS A SHOT AT SOMETHING MORE... PROFESSIONAL?
HOW SHOULD I KNOW? HERE, ASK AARON. HE'S ALWAYS HERE SCOUTING TALENT FOR RCA AND OTHER LABELS.

JOPLIN? HELL YEAH!! THAT BROAD'S GOT A GIFT. I'VE BEEN BADGERING RCA TO AUDITION HER FOR TWO WEEKS!

SHE'S GOT THE VOICE, THE TALENT, THE BALLS... YOU CAN ALWAYS PICK 'EM, LEO, JANIS AND ALL THE OTHERS! THAT'S WHY I ALWAYS HANG OUT HERE, HAHA.
SHE LIKES HER BOOZE, TOO, FROM WHAT I COULD TELL.

YEAH, THAT TOO... IT'S KIND OF A PROBLEM ACTUALLY.

WHAT DO YOU MEAN?
WE ALL DRINK A LITTLE, NO HARM NO FOUL. BUT JANIS GOES FOR ANYTHING SHE CAN GET DRINK, EAT, SMOKE, SNIFF, SUCK, CHEW, LORD KNOWS WHAT ELSE.
NO SELF-CONTROL WHATSOEVER, SHE CAN'T HELP IT. MIGHT MAKE HER IMPOSSIBLE TO MANAGE.
49

If only you had reined in those impulses, sweetheart...
POLICE DEPT
BERKELEY CALIF.
19433
2 21 63

YOU'RE IN THE SYSTEM NOW, YOUNG LADY.
SHOPLIFTING. WE WON'T BOOK YOU, BUT IF WE CATCH YOU AGAIN...

But self-control wasn't your thing, honey...

WH-WHAT THE HELL! LET GO OF ME, YOU MORONS!! WH-WHAT... WHERE... OH, SHIIIIIIIIIT.....

Your thing was spontaneity. Always and fully.

OOOOW!

Whatever the cost....

SHUT YOUR PIE HOLE, YOU SKANK!

NO, YOU SHUT *YOUR* PIE HOLE!

YOU THINK I'M SCARED OF YOU, ASSHOLE?

JANIS, PLEASE, CALM DOWN...

50

MAYBE YOU'RE NOT SCARED OF ME, BITCH....
...BUT WHEN I'M DONE WITH YOU...
NO!
WHAT'S THAT, BITCH? I CAN'T HEAR YOU!
STOP IT!! PLEASE! STOP!
PLEASE CALL AN AMBULANCE! HURRY! SHE NEEDS MEDICAL ATTENTION!
You got lucky that time. It could nave been worse...
WHO WAS THAT ASSHOLE?
BEATING UP A WOMAN... SHIT, MAN.
THIS IS THE THIRD TIME THIS MONTH SHE PICKED A FIGHT...
SHE'S A TROUBLEMAKER!
TAKE HER TO THE HOSPITAL AND GOOD RIDDANCE!
51
But it didn't help your image...

YES... YES... HA, HA... YESSSS!! AGAIN, HONEY... AGAIN... YES, YES, LIKE THAT... DON'T STOP... YESS... AAAHH!
You took some breaks, of course.
The body does need attention.
I ADORE YOU, SWEETHEART... I ADORE YOU... HIT ME UP WITH SOME MORE CRANK... IT'S SOOO GOOD...
Pleasure was always in your blood. In whatever shape or form.
YESSSS.... YES... YES! HARDER... HARDER... AGAIN... YESSSS... FUCK ME... THAT'S RIGHT... YES... FUCK ME!
FUCK, THAT WAS AMAZING! HONESTLY, I'M NOT SURE WHICH I LIKE BETTER... SCREWING OR DOPE, HA HA HA!
OH, OKAY. SO YOU DON'T LIKE ME MORE.
I LOVE TO GET HIGH TOO, DARLING.
EVEN THOUGH RIGHT NOW, I'M RUNNING REAL LOW ON SPEED AND SMACK.
BENZEDRINE TABLETS
YOU'RE BROKE? WHAT ABOUT YOUR MUSIC? DON'T YOU PASS THE HAT AROUND?
PFF. THOSE ASSHOLES. I'M READY TO GO BACK ON TONIGHT! BUT APPARENTLY I'M TROUBLE... I'M A NUISANCE...

A nomadic lifestyle. Always on the move. Like the Beats...
And that, honey, became your routine your first few months in San Francisco.
METHEDRINE
Equal parts ecstasy and danger.

HEY, JANIS !

IT'S BEEN MONTHS!
HEY, CHET... MONTHS, REALLY?

SOME OF US HAVE BEEN WORRIED ABOUT YOU LATELY...
WORRIED? WHY? I HAVE SCADS OF LOVERS AND A JOB AT AMERICAN CAN TO KEEP ME GOING.

SO NAH, I'M FINE, CHET.
HMM. YOU SURE ABOUT THAT?

LISTEN, JANIS, SING THAT TUNE ALL YOU WANT, BUT... JUST EASE UP A BIT, WILL YOU? SLOW DOWN. PLEASE...

NAH, DON'T WORRY. I'M FINE. REALLY.

ALL RIGHT, SEE YA, CHET..
54

JANIS!! NICE OF YOU TO FINALLY VISIT!

PASSING THROUGH PORT ARTHUR ISN'T EASY, YOU KNOW, LAURA. I HAVE MY JOB IN FRISCO, MY, UM... MY CAREER, ALL THAT.

YOU CAN'T BLAME YOUR SISTER. IT'S GREAT THAT YOU CAME HOME FOR CHRISTMAS, BUT... WE MISS YOU.
Merry Christmas 1963
DON'T YOU MISS OUR BEAUTIFUL TEXAS?
I KNOW, DAD, I KNOW... BUT ANYWAY, IT SURE IS GREAT TO SEE EVERYONE AGAIN!

MISS IT? HELL NO I DON'T MISS IT! ESPECIALLY NOT AFTER WHAT JUST HAPPENED IN DALLAS! BUNCH OF MURDERERS!
KILLING KENNEDY... BASTARDS!
JANIS!! HOW DARE YOU...?

HERE WE GO AGAIN...
IT'S STRONGER THAN THE TWO OF YOU, ISN'T IT? BARELY BACK TOGETHER AND YOU'RE DOWN EACH OTHER'S THROATS ALREADY! GOOD LORD.
55

HOLY SHIT!! I DON'T HOW YOU NEW YORKERS CAN STAND THESE SUMMERS! IT'S NOT EVEN THIS HOT IN THE DEVIL'S ASS!
HA! YEP, THIS ISN'T FRISCO, THAT'S FOR SURE! BUT HEY, YOU WANTED TO SEE NEW YORK, HONEY, RIGHT? WELL, WELCOME TO THE LOWER EAST SIDE, BABY!
DAMN... IT'S NOT EVEN SEVEN IN THE MORNING AND MY THROAT IS ALREADY PARCHED...
WE CAN GO TO THE BAR DOWNSTAIRS. THEY OPEN AT SIX.
GETTING LIQUORED UP AT SEVEN A.M.... THAT'S SOMETHING, HUH?
HA, HA, YEAH, IT'S GREAT!
HOW LONG HAS IT BEEN SINCE WE LAST SLEPT?
DON'T WORRY ABOUT IT. WE'RE HAVING FUN, AREN'T WE?
ALL RIGHT. THREE BOURBONS TO GET THINGS STARTED.
JANIS! YOUR USUAL SOUTHERN COMFORT?
OLD RELIABLE
56

walkin' the dog Just walkin'

DOES SHE EVER SLOW DOWN?

NOPE. NEVER.

HEY TOUGH GUYS! ANY OF YOU WANNA SHOOT POOL WITH A TEXAS GIRL?

CAREFUL, SWEETIE... YOU'RE ASKIN' FOR IT!

HA, HA. LET'S GO, GET OUT YOUR STICK, CHAMP!

WAIT TILL YOU SEE THIS. SHE MIGHT NOT LOOK LIKE IT, BUT SHE ALWAYS BEATS THEM. THE SAME EXACT WAY.

Walking the Dog © Rufus Thomas, 1963.

Slugs
Slugs'

KIND OF A CRUMMY VIBE IN HERE TONIGHT, HUH?
TELL ME ABOUT IT. EVEN IF I HAD FEATHERS COMING OUT MY ASS NOBODY WOULD'VE LISTENED.

DON'T BE BLUE, HONEY. THINGS WILL TURN AROUND. IN THE MEANTIME, AT LEAST YOU HAVE THAT DAY JOB WITH THE PHONE COMPANY.
UH-HUH... I'M NOT SO SURE ABOUT NEW YORK ANYMORE... RACE RIOTS IN HARLEM LAST MONTH, FINICKY AUDIENCES...
I MEAN, IT'S EASY TO SCORE SPEED AND DOPE HERE, WHICH IS GROOVY... BUT IT'S BEEN FOUR MONTHS ALREADY. SHOULDN'T WE JUST HEAD HOME, LINDA?

DRIVE SAFE AND KEEP IN TOUCH, GIRLS!
...
TO FRISCO! FLOOR IT!

58

Down Hearted Blues © Alberta Hunger and Lovie Austin, 1922.

Strange Fruit, © Lewis Allen (Abel Meeropol), 1939

You sometimes got so close, sweetheart...
JANIS!
KENAI!
I want to hold your hand
Fame and glory seemed almost within reach...

I'M SO GLAD YOU CAME, JANIS! TONIGHT'S GONNA BE GAS, YOU'LL SEE. ALL THE IMPORTANT ARTISTS ARE HERE! COME, I'LL INTRODUCE YOU.
Oh Pretty Woman

DAVE, DAVE, YOU HAVE TO MEET MY GOOD FRIEND JANIS! JANIS, DAVID CROSBY. THE WHOLE WORLD'S TALKING ABOUT HIS MUSIC.

JANIS IS AN INCREDIBLE VOCALIST, DAVE, AND--
YES, WE'VE MET BEFORE, IF MEMORY SERVES!
WE SANG ON THE SAME STAGE LAST YEAR. AT THE COFFEE GALLERY OR SOMEWHERE.
THAT'S RIGHT! HOW'S TRICKS, DAVID?

WELL, I'M IN A BAND WITH TWO CATS FROM L.A. JIM MCGUINN AND GENE CLARK. WE'RE THE JET SET. AND IT'S GOING PRETTY WELL.
OUR MANAGER, JIM DICKSON, GOT HIS HANDS ON A NEW DYLAN SONG HE WANTS US TO RECORD.
61

DYLAN?! WOW, THAT'S FAR OUT, MAN. I'M HAPPY FOR YOU, REALLY.
YEAH, I DON'T KNOW. WE'RE DEBATING...
YOU'RE *DEBATING?!*
LAUNCHING WITH A COVER SONG, I DUNNO... MAYBE WE SHOULD GET OUR OWN SONGS OUT THERE INSTEAD...
I get around huhu hu h
round round round
YOU'RE RIGHT, IT'S IMPORTANT TO DO YOUR OWN STUFF. BUT DYLAN, I MEAN, COME ON...
SORRY FOR INTERRUPTING, YOU TWO, BUT I SEE SOMEONE ELSE JANIS REALLY NEEDS TO MEET.
AND WHAT'S THE NAME OF THE NEW DYLAN SONG?
MR TAMBOURINE MAN.
The house of the rising sun
WHAT A COINCIDENCE: WE'RE TALKING TO DAVE ABOUT DYLAN AND HERE'S SOMEONE WHO RECORDED WITH ZIMBO IN THE STUDIO.
HEY, MIKE, WHAT'S UP, MAN? I WANT YOU TO MEET A REALLY PROMISING VOCALIST, MY GOOD FRIEND JANIS.
JANIS, THIS IS MICHAEL BLOOMFIELD.
You really
You really got me

HEY, JANIS. I GOTTA SAY, KENAI'S A REAL ACE AT BRINGING TALENTED PEOPLE TOGETHER...
YOU'LL SEE, MIKE, JANIS HAS AN INCREDIBLE VOICE. THANKS TO ME, REALLY: WE USED TO LIVE TOGETHER AND I INTRODUCED HER TO EDITH PIAF.
Time is on my side
YEAH, MAN, PIAF. LOVE HER. SO MIKE, I HEARD YOU JAMMED WITH DYLAN?
A LITTLE, YEAH. BUT NOWADAYS, I'M PLAYING THE BLUES WITH TWO BUDDIES FROM CHICAGO, PAUL BUTTERFIELD AND ELVIN BISHOP. WE START RECORDING IN DECEMBER.
THE BLUES?! I REALLY DIG THE BLUES, MAN!! I MYSELF--
FRIENDS, WE GOT SOME CRYSTAL THAT JUST CAME IN, IT'S IN THE KITCHEN, IF YOU WANT.
Dancing street
A Hard Day's Night
HA, HA, YOU KNOW HOW TO TALK TO THE LADIES, BABY! I'M COMING!
See the
funny
ittle clow
But it didn't take much to wake up your demons...
63

And then there were days the color of night, sweetheart...
WHAT THE... WH... WHAT THE... WHO... WHO DID...
HEY!! WHO THE HELL ARE YOU, BITCH?
GET OUTTA MY HOME! THIS... THIS IS MY HOME!
AAAAAH! STOP IT, STOP IT!
OK, OK, I'M LEAVING. LOOK, MAN, I'M LEAVING.
BUT, UM, YOU GOT ANY SPARE CHANGE, BROTHER?
64

The SALVATION ARMY
Memorial Hotel
CLEAN ROOMS ELEVATOR
CANTEEN SHOWER LAUNDRY
ROOMS for DAY SLEEPERS
IS THIS THE SOUP KITCHEN?

YEP. GOTTA GET IN LINE. LIKE EVERYBODY ELSE

WHAT ARE YOU DOING HERE, KID? YOU DON'T LOOK OLD ENOUGH TO HAVE FALLEN SO LOW.

UM... JUST GOING THROUGH A ROUGH TIME... IT'S TEMPORARY. I, UM... I'M ACTUALLY A SINGER, SEE. I'LL BE BACK IN THE SADDLE IN TWO, THREE WEEKS TOP. FOR SURE.

...DEFINITELY...
65

300→
SOUTH VAN NESS
HEY HONEY, HOW ABOUT SOME REASONABLY PRICED SMACK?
MARKET WINES
LIQUOR
LIQUORS GROCERIES
LIQUORS
YOU SURE YOU WANNA DO THAT, DOLL? D'YOU SEE WHERE YOU ARE?

I'VE GOT SPEED TOO, IF YOU PREFER.

LOOK, I'M NOT USUALLY ONE TO SAY NO TO A LITTLE BUZZ, BUT IN YOUR CASE... HERE, TAKE THIS....

AND DO ME A FAVOR. GET A CRIB FOR THE NIGHT AND SOBER UP.

OTHERWISE, THIS CITY'S GONNA GET YOU.
AND SOONER THAN YOU THINK.

66

GOODNESS, I'D FORGOTTEN HOW SHORT THE DAYS ARE UP HERE IN THE NORTH.

IT'S JUST BARELY FIVE AND IT'S ALMOST DARK OUT.

NO LEFT TURN

IT'S WINTER, DAD.

I'LL SAY! HOW CAN YOU LIVE IN SUCH A COLD CLIMATE?

TWO COFFEES, NICE AND HOT PLEASE, MISS. AND WE'LL PROBABLY GET SOMETHING TO EAT, TOO.

I'M THINKING.... A GOOD MEAL MIGHT HIT THE SPOT, RIGHT?

LISTEN, JANIS... I... FAR BE IT FROM ME TO INTERFERE IN YOUR LIFE CHOICES, YOU KNOW THAT...

YOU WERE PRECOCIOUS AND I BELIEVE WE'VE ALWAYS LET YOU FOLLOW YOUR OWN PATH...

YOU... YOU AND I HAVE ALWAYS RESPECTED EACH OTHER.

AND I INTEND TO KEEP IT THAT WAY...

SO... TAKE WHAT I'M SAYING FOR WHAT IT'S WORTH, AND....

...JUST TAKE CARE OF YOURSELF, OKAY?

I'M BEGGING YOU.

HEY, MARGARETA... HOW ARE YOU, GORGEOUS...
KAUKONEN
Occasionally, you would get back on your feet...
HEY, JANIS. HE'S ALREADY ON STAGE. WAITING FOR YOU.
I HAVE TO GO. I NEED TO TYPE UP A FAMILY LETTER.
When you did, anyone could see and hear that the flame was still burning inside you...
The talent of others had the power to awaken yours...
TIDING TIDING
JORMA! MY HERO!
TELL ME AGAIN?
THE TANGENT IN PALO ALTO, NEXT FRIDAY. ONE HOUR ON STAGE AND WE CAN PLAY WHAT WE WANT.
THIS TIME, WE'RE RECORDING IT. IT'LL HELP US IMPROVE.
SONY
WANNA START WITH *TROUBLE IN MIND?*
PERFECT.
68

Trouble in Mind, © Richard M. Jones, 1924

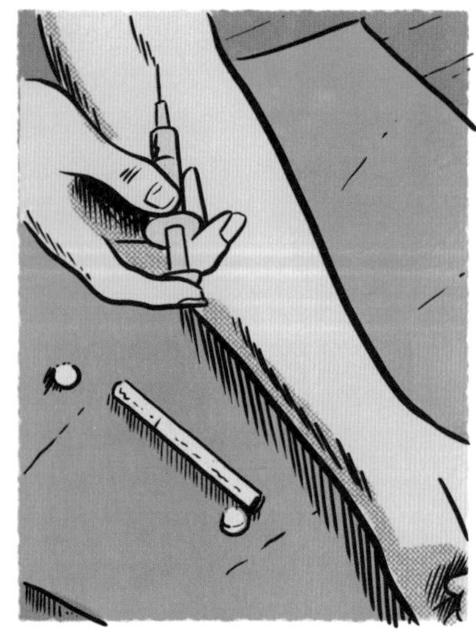

FRIENDS, THANK YOU ALL FOR BEING HERE! AS YOU KNOW, THIS NIGHT IS ALL ABOUT JANIS...

JANIS REALLY WANTS TO GO HOME TO PORT ARTHUR TO SEE HER FAMILY. BUT UNFORTUNATELY, HER FINANCES AT THE MOMENT ARE A BIT... LIMITED...

SO WE DISCUSSED IT, AND WE FIGURED THAT BY BANDING TOGETHER, WE, YOU, EVERYONE, ARE GOING TO COLLECTIVELY BUY HER A BUS TICKET HOME.

SUNSHINE, WHO YOU ALL KNOW, WILL BE TAKING UP THE COLLECTION. THANK YOU, FRIENDS! AND IF YOU'RE GOOD, MAYBE JANIS WILL SING US A COUPLE OF GREAT SONGS...
70

Nobody Knows You When You're Down and Out, © Jimmy Cox, 1923

THE UNIVERSITY OF THE STATE OF TEXAS
EDUCATION DEPARTMENT
BERNARD GIARRITANO
PSYCHOLOGIST
HOW ARE YOU FEELING TODAY, JANIS?

I MEAN... MY FAMILY'S TRIED TO BE SUPPORTIVE SINCE I GOT BACK, AND I KNOW I'M LUCKY, BUT...
IT'S STILL... VERY DIFFICULT.

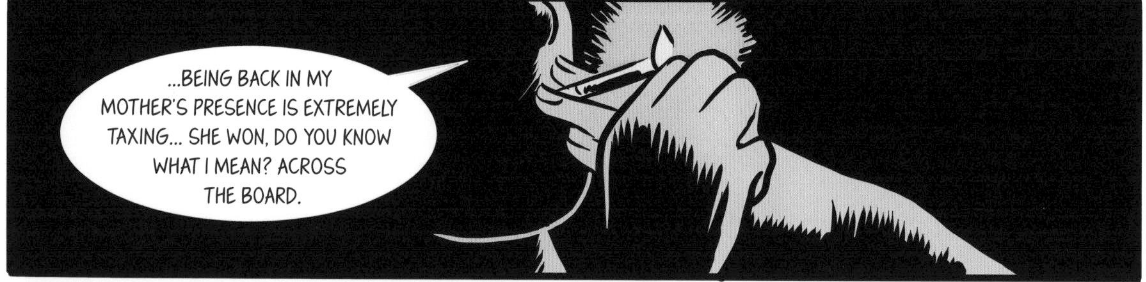
...BEING BACK IN MY MOTHER'S PRESENCE IS EXTREMELY TAXING... SHE WON, DO YOU KNOW WHAT I MEAN? ACROSS THE BOARD.

IT'S COMPLICATED. I... I THINK THAT BREAKING WITH MY FORMER LIFE HAS BEEN BENEFICIAL TO ME, ESPECIALLY PHYSICALLY... BUT AT THE SAME TIME... I FEEL LIKE MY LIGHT IS GOING OUT.

DIDN'T YOU TELL ME YOU WERE THINKING ABOUT GOING BACK TO SCHOOL?
72

CHERYL, DID I TELL YOU JANIS IS GOING BACK TO SCHOOL?

NOOO! WELL THAT'S JUST GROOVY! WHAT WILL YOU MAJOR IN, JANIS?

I ENROLLED AT LAMAR. IN SOCIOLOGY AND HISTORY.
FANTASTIC!
THAT'S RIGHT. FANTASTIC.

AND IN THE MEANTIME, SETH AND I WILL DO EVERYTHING WE CAN TO FIND HER A JOB.
A JOB AS A SECRETARY WOULD BE A GOOD OPTION. TO START WITH, OF COURSE.

WHAT WOULD YOU LADIES SAY TO A NICE CUP OF TEA?
TEA! YEAH, BABY! SUPER!

LAURA, WATCH YOUR LANGUAGE! HOW DO YOU EXPECT TO EVER ATTRACT A HUSBAND IF YOU TALK LIKE A TRUCK DRIVER?!
73

AND WHERE ARE YOU AT WITH YOUR... ADDICTIONS?
I QUIT EVERYTHING!! I'VE DONE A LOT OF DRUGS, TRUST ME... I KNOW WHAT A SLIPPERY SLOPE THAT IS...
TELL ME.
THE WORST PART,
IS THE LUCIDITY YOU GET WITH SPEED. EVERYTHING SEEMS SO CLEAR.
ON SOME DAYS, IN FRISCO, I FOUND THAT ACUITY ALMOST UNBEARABLE.
EVEN HEROIN CAN BE INTENSELY... CALMING...
AND THAT'S PAINFUL?
OF COURSE!! BECAUSE DEEP DOWN, NONE OF THAT IS REAL!
IN THE END, IT'S THE BODY THAT PAYS THE PRICE...
AND IT'S A STEEP ONE!
THE THOUGHT OF USING AGAIN TERRIFIES ME, YOU KNOW. IT'S AN... UNBEARABLE PROSPECT. I REALLY, REALLY WANT TO BECOME NORMAL!
74

WHAT ABOUT YOUR LOVE LIFE, JANIS? ANYTHING COMFORTING IN THAT AREA?

SIGH EVEN THAT PART IS PATHETIC... AND I LOVE SEX...

SOMETIMES I THINK I MIGHT JUST BE... UNFIT... UNFIT FOR EVERYTHING... MAYBE THAT'S WHY I LOVE BESSIE SMITH AND BILLIE HOLIDAY SO MUCH. THEY DIDN'T FIT IN EITHER...

I AGREE WITH YOU WHAT YOU SAY ABOUT YOUR PAIN AND YOUR MALAISE, WITHOUT QUESTION. BUT I WOULD BE MORE RESERVED ABOUT YOUR CHOICE TO LEAD WHAT YOU CALL A "NORMAL LIFE..."

I WONDER IF PERHAPS YOU SHOULDN'T CONSIDER RESUMING AN ARTISTIC ACTIVITY...

YOU MIGHT FIND THAT LIBERATING. PAINTING? SINGING?

OH MY GOD! THE DRUGS THOUGH....

SO THAT'S INEVITABLE?

...IN BEAUMONT, WHERE I HAD THE OPPORTUNITY TO HEAR A YOUNG WOMAN I CONSIDER TO BE...
TAP TAP TAP

...THE BEST BLUES SINGER IN THE COUNTRY. HER NAME IS JANIS JOPLIN.
TAP TAP TAP TAP TAP

JIM LANGDON! ENOUGH WITH THE HYPERBOLA! YOU FLATTER ME...
I SHOULD INTRODUCE YOU TO MY EDITOR-IN-CHIEF, THEN! HE RAILS ON ME TOO FOR CHAMPIONING A VOCALIST NOBODY'S EVER HEARD OF!

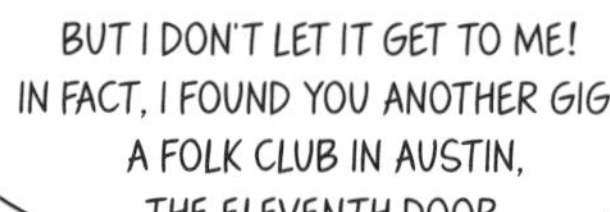
BUT I DON'T LET IT GET TO ME! IN FACT, I FOUND YOU ANOTHER GIG. A FOLK CLUB IN AUSTIN, THE ELEVENTH DOOR.

YOU SURE THAT'S A GOOD IDEA, JIM? IT'S TEMPTING, BUT... YOU KNOW HOW FREAKED OUT I AM ABOUT SLIPPING BACK INTO MY OLD WAYS...

76

NOW YOU LISTEN TO ME, JIM LANGDON! IF YOU THINK I'M GOING TO LET YOU RUIN JANIS'S LIFE, YOU ARE SORELY MISTAKEN, I'M TELLING YOU THAT RIGHT NOW!

YOU'VE WRITTEN ABOUT HER THREE TIMES NOW IN YOUR NEWSPAPER, AND I DO NOT CARE FOR WHAT I READ!

JANIS IS NOT A SINGER ANYMORE, DO YOU HEAR ME?! SHE CAME BACK TO TEXAS TO START A NEW LIFE AND IT IS OUT OF THE QUESTION FOR HER TO RELAPSE AND LOSE HER WAY AGAIN!

HER ENTIRE FAMILY HAS COME TOGETHER TO HELP HER CONFRONT HER DEMONS, AND WE WILL NOT LET YOU LEAD HER DOWN A PATH THAT NEARLY KILLED HER ONCE ALREADY!

YOU ARE HURTING JANIS, MR. LANGDON!! I WOULD THEREFORE ASK YOU TO PLEASE STOP WRITING ABOUT HER AT ONCE!

CLIC

77

SO, GETTING YOU TO START SINGING AGAIN WASN'T SUCH A BAD THING AFTER ALL, RIGHT?
RIGHT. YOU WERE RIGHT! AND NOW, I FEEL READY TO START SINGING PROFESSIONALLY.

THESE GUYS ARE GREAT, HUH? AND I DIG THE NAME! 13TH FLOOR ELEVATORS...
YEAH, THEY'RE GROOVY! ESPECIALLY ROCKY ERICKSON AND TOMMY HALL... THEY SORT OF OFFERED ME TO SING WITH THEM, YOU KNOW.
You're gonna miss me

AND...?
I DUNNO. I'M NOT SURE YET. YOU KNOW ME, CAN YOU PICTURE ME IN A BAND?

ONLY YOU CAN DECIDE, JANIS. ALL I CAN TELL YOU, IS: FOLLOW YOUR INSTINCT! IT WON'T FAIL YOU.
78

MOTEL
Fine Motel
HEY, TRAVIS RIVERS... I HEARD YOU WERE IN TOWN, HONEY, AND THAT YOU WANTED TO SEE ME. SO HERE I AM!
JANIS! HOW LONG'S IT BEEN?! THREE, FOUR YEARS?
I'D SAY 1961. DURING THE GHETTO DAYS.
COME ON, LET'S GO GRAB A DRINK! THERE'S A NEARBY JOINT CALLED CHEZ FRED, AND IF I'M NOT MISTAKEN, BOZ SCAGGS IS PLAYING TONIGHT.
Chez Fred
WHAT?!! SAY THAT AGAIN...
IT WAS CHET'S IDEA. HE MANAGES THIS BAND OF CATS THAT CALL THEMSELVES BIG BROTHER AND THE HOLDING COMPANY. THINGS ARE STARTING TO HAPPEN... BUT THE VOCALS AREN'T QUITE THERE YET.
AND RIGHT NOW, IN FRISCO, ALL THE COOLEST BANDS HAVE A FEMALE VOCALIST...
SO CHET THOUGHT ABOUT YOU AND THE GUYS AGREED TO LET YOU AUDITION FOR THEM. RETURN BUS FARE GUARANTEED IF THINGS DON'T WORK OUT.
IF YOU'RE INTO IT, OF COURSE.
ARE YOU KIDDING?
MAN... THIS IS *EXACTLY* WHAT I DREAM OF DOING!
79

GIVING UP YOUR TRAINING AS A FUTURE SCHOOLTEACHER? ARE YOU SURE ABOUT THIS, MISS JOPLIN?

YES, SIR, I... I THINK SO.
BESIDES, IT'S JUST A TRIAL PERIOD, YOU KNOW... IF IT DOESN'T WORK OUT, I'LL BE BACK IN A FEW WEEKS.

HMM... AND HOW DID YOUR FAMILY REACT?

OH, THEY APPROVE, OF COURSE!
THEY APPROVE...
VERY WELL, IF THAT'S REALLY WHAT YOU WANT... GOOD LUCK THEN, MISS...

CHET, BABY, WE GOT A GOOD CATCH! I'M BRINGING BACK JANIS FOR THE AUDITION! A GREAT CATCH EVEN, 'CAUSE... WELL JANIS IS NOT TIMID, AND FRANKLY, THAT'S FINE WITH ME...
80

ROY'S
VACANCY
MOTEL
CAFE

COURT

REMEMBER THIS DAY, JANIS: JUNE 4TH, 1966! FOR ALL WE KNOW, THIS MIGHT BE THE DAY THAT LAUNCHES YOU AS A STAR...
82

CHAPTER 3

Spells and Charms

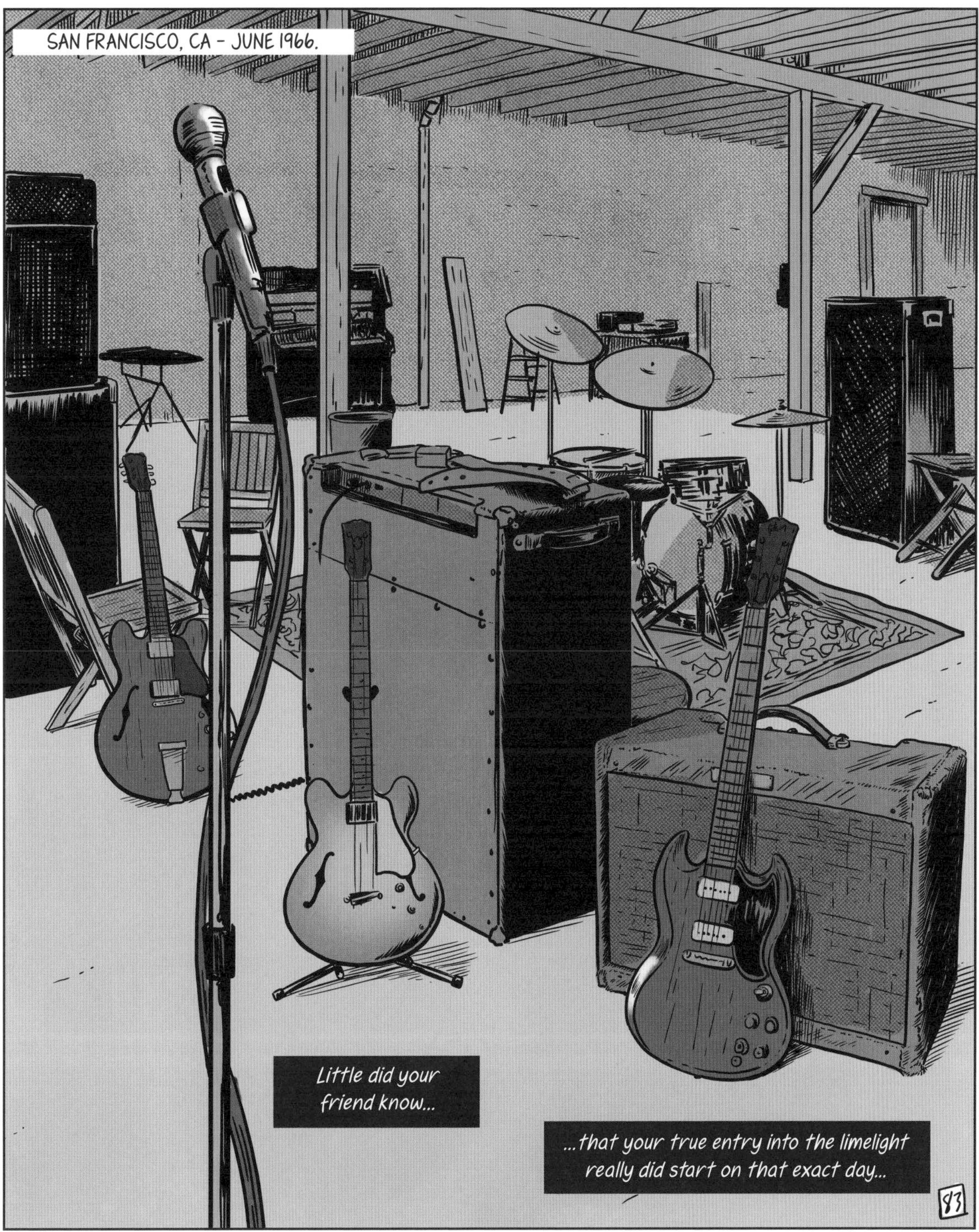

SAN FRANCISCO, CA - JUNE 1966.
Little did your friend know...
...that your true entry into the limelight really did start on that exact day...
83

HA HA HA! HOLY SHIT, TRAVIS, THEY SAID I'M IN!
Four men had chosen you, gorgeous... With no pressure, of their own free will.
Dave Getz on the drums.
James Gurley on guitar.
Peter Albin on bass.
Sam Andrew on guitar.
84

Nothing on earth energized you like that did! On June 10, less than a week after your return, you five were already performing on the stage at the Avalon Ballroom...
AVALON
TOW AWAY ZONE NO STOPPING
STARTING TONIGHT, BIG BROTHER AND THE HOLDING COMPANY HAVE A NEW VOCALIST, AND HER NAME IS JANIS JOPLIN!
Big Brother & The Holding Co.
It was a night that everyone in that room remembered forever...
85

ar Mother . . .
Your beautiful letter
came today & prodded
guilt feeling once a
so here I am . . .
WE FOUND A GREAT COTTAGE IN WHICH WE CAN ALL WORK AND LIVE TOGETHER.
I'M SETTLED INTO MY NEW ROOM...
...AND NOW I'M SITTING NICE AND COZY BY THE FIREPLACE...
...WITH TALL DOORS OPEN ON A 180-DEGREE VIEW OF THE SEQUOIAS ALL AROUND US. IT'S BEAUTIFUL.
I think life in the country is going to be great for us.
86

We work on our music a lot, of course, and I enjoy that so much...
The boys are like peacocks! They all have hair as long as the Beatles'. They wear tight, low cut pants...
DAMN IT, MAN, CAN YOU PLEASE QUIT THAT CRAP?
...very loud shirts: prints, high collars, large sleeves... over the top, basically!
YOU KNOW WHAT I WENT THROUGH TO GET CLEAN.
SEEING YOU PASS AROUND SMACK IS FREAKING ME OUT.
SORRY, JANIS... WE'LL BE MORE CAREFUL, I PROMISE.
YEAH, YOU'D BETTER...
87

The Grateful Dead, another band from the Bay region, live nearby...

DORRIS
97
ALTURAS
It all started falling into place...
Gradually, and under the best circumstances...
The Frisco and Bay club circuit-- the California Hall, the Filmore, the Avalon, and even beyond San Jose, all the way to Monterey...
UREKA
5
REDDING
NEVADA
YUBA CITY
You were holding your demons at bay...
SAN FRANCISCO
SANTA CRU
MONTEREY
...well, most of them...
OS ANGELES
JOSHUA
PALM SPRINGS
ANAHEIM
SANTA ANA
Fate even had the good sense of putting someone in your path you needed to meet...
15
89
5
ESCONDIDO
8
SAN DIEGO
TIJUANA

Big mama Thornton
OH MY GOD, I *HAVE* TO TALK TO HER...
HOLY SHIT, JAMES, THIS BIG MAMA PLAYS MY FAVORITE KINDA MUSIC!
I LOVED *BALL AND CHAIN*! IT WAS SO MOVING!
THANKS, HONEY!
WOULD YOU... WOULD YOU MIND IF I DID A COVER OF THAT SONG?
OH, YOU WOULDN'T BE THE FIRST TO SING ONE OF MY SONGS, KID...
JUST PROMISE ME ONE THING: SING IT IN A WAY THAT NOBODY WILL EVER FORGET THAT SONG.
90

Down on Me
YOU'RE THE ONE WHO WANTED TO COME HERE. WE'RE BOOKED FOR FOUR WEEKS, JANIS. THAT'S UNHEARD OF!
THANKS FOR COMING TONIGHT.
Mother blues
SERIOUSLY, GUYS, WHAT THE HELL ARE WE DOING HERE?
AND IN CHICAGO, TO BOOT... YOU *LOVE* THE BLUES!
OKAY, BUT... HAVE YOU CHECKED OUT THE AUDIENCE? THE SAN FRANCISCO SOUND... YEAH RIGHT... I DON'T THINK THEY'RE DIGGING IT.
PLUS, STICKING US WITH A DANCER TO DRAW THEM IN...
HEY GUYS, WHAT'S HAPPENING?
BOB SHAD! WHAT THE HELL ARE YOU DOING HERE, MAN?
WELL, THIS IS MY HOME TURF. YOU AUDITIONED FOR ME IN FRISCO, BUT I'M FROM DETROIT.
I JUST HEARD YOUR SET. LOVED IT! AND SINCE YOU ALL SEEM A LITTLE LOST, I HAVE A SUGGESTION...

OUR SUMMER GIG WITH MOTHER BLUES ISN'T LOOKING GOD. BUT BOB SHAD SAID WE SHOULD RECORD AN ALBUM, INSTEAD.
RIGHT NOW, AT THE UNITED STUDIOS. AND UNDER CONTRACT WITH HIS LABEL, MAINSTREAM. WHAT DO YOU THINK, CHET?
IT'S UP TO YOU GUYS. PERSONALLY, I DON'T THINK SHAD IS RELIABLE. AND OUTSIDE OF CHICAGO AND DETROIT, NOBODY'S HEARD OF MAINSTREAM RECORDS.
SO, WHAT DID THE BIG CHET HELMS SAY?
NOT TOO KEEN ON IT. HE SAYS HE'S UNCOOL.
BUT WHY, PETER? WHY?! WE'RE TALKING ABOUT A FREAKING ALBUM, DAMN IT!! I MEAN, ISN'T THAT FAR OUT?
LETTER OF INTENT
between MAINSTREAM RECORDS, INC. 1290 Avenue of the Americas, New York, New York; and PETER ALBIN, DAVID GETZ, JAMES GURLEY, JANICE JOPLIN and SAM ANDREW, performing as BIG BROTHER AND THE HOLDING COMPANY.
MAINSTREAM RECORDS, INC. shall record the group for a period of one year from date with 3 options of one year each subject to terms and conditions to be defined later at a royalty rate of 5%. Formal contracts will be prepared and entered into by the parties within the next 10 days.
MAINSTREAM RECORDS, INC.
By
BIG BROTHER AND THE HOLDING COMPANY
Dated: Sept 7 1966
THERE! WE'RE IN BUSINESS, BUDDY! FOR FIVE YEARS!
92

WHAT KINDA SOUND DO YOU WANT, BOB? WHAT'S THE TONE?
ALL RIGHT, GUYS! HIT IT!
DON'T WORRY ABOUT THE TONE, WE'LL HANDLE THAT IN MIXING. NOW HIT IT!
OK... HE MUST KNOW WHAT HE'S DOING... ALL RIGHT, JANIS, GO!
I HAVE A WEIRD FEELING... LIKE THAT RECORDING WASN'T REAL... STRANGE, HUH?
YEAH... I THINK WE MADE THE WRONG DECISION...
STEREO
MAINSTREAM
BIG BROTHER & THE HOLDING COMPANY
In the end, that first album only came out a year later, when your band was finally doing well. Shad knew what he was doing...

OTIS REDDING
& HIS ORCHESTRA
FILLMORE AUDITORIUM
$3.00

RIGHT HERE. THIS SHOULD BE PERFECT.

I'M NOT MOVING FROM THIS SPOT ALL NIGHT!

SORRY, JUST CURIOUS: WHAT EXACTLY ARE YOU TRYING TO DO?
FIND THE PERFECT SPOT, MAN!

I'VE BEEN HERE EVERY DAY SINCE TUESDAY!

AND FOR OTIS'S LAST CONCERT IN FRISCO, I WANT THE PERFECT ACOUSTICS AND LINE OF SIGHT!
94

Shake. © Sam Cooke, 1964

HOLY SHIT, LINDA.... I CAN'T BELIEVE YOU WERE MARRIED TO PAT CASSIDY... ONE OF MY BEAT HEROES!
In the spring of '67, you met Linda Gravenites.
HOW ABOUT THIS EMBROIDERED SHIRT? IT WOULD LOOK GREAT ON YOU...
AND DON'T FORGET: THAT PURSE HAS TO BE BIG ENOUGH TO HOLD AT LEAST ONE BOOK AND ONE BOTTLE!
This talented and intuitive stylist became your roommate on Lyon Street, your confidant...
...and the one who showed you the importance of something you weren't doing yet: cultivating a look.
TA-DAAAAAAM!
ASHBURY STREET
FAR OUT!
You were gradually finding your vibe... your character...
It wasn't true happiness quite yet, sweetheart...
CHECK IT OUT, GENE ANTHONY JUST SENT ME HIS PHOTO FROM LAST FEBRUARY, IN FRONT OF THE GRATEFUL DEAD'S HOUSE: BIG BROTHER, QUICKSILVER, THE CHARLATANS, JEFFERSON AIRPLANE... IT'S THE WHOLE FRISCO ROCK SCENE... AND YOU!
...but it was starting to look like it.

MONTEREY
INTERNATIONAL
POP FESTIVAL
JUNE 16 • 17 • 18
And then, a little later that year, in the early summer, there was that extraordinary moment...
PEANUTS
The poster itself was stunning...
...and the audience was especially receptive....
FREE YAWF LEADERS JAILED FOR AIDING ANTI-WAR G.I.s
OTIS REDDING, HENDRIX, SIMON & GARFUNKEL, THE WHO, THE BYRDS, AIRPLANE... EVERYONE'S HERE!
WHO'S BIG BROTHER?
OH, I KNOW THOSE GUYS, I SAW THEM AT THE MATRIX IN FRISCO. WAIT TILL YOU HEAR THEIR LEAD VOCALIST, SHE'S BITCHEN!
97

<cocktails>
HOLY SHIT, BOYS! I'M DIGGING THIS PLACE!
CAN YOU BELIEVE WHAT'S HAPPENING TO US?!
WE'RE FREAKING PLAYING HERE TOMORROW!! AND ALL THE BIG NAMES IN MUSIC ARE HERE!
THOSE GUYS EVEN CAME FROM ENGLAND: ERIC BURDON & THE ANIMALS.
SIMON & GARFUNKEL.
LET'S GET OUT
BUT THE BIGGEST BIG SHOT, MY DARLINGS, IS THAT GUY THERE: ALBERT GROSSMAN HE MANAGES DYLAN, PETER PAUL & MARY, ODETTA, JOHN LEE HOOKER, AND SCADS OF OTHERS. WE HAVE TO TALK TO HIM.

MONTEREY INTERNATIONAL POP MUSIC FESTIVAL - '67
JUNE 17 1967
FRIDAY 9:00 P.M.
MONTEREY COUNTY FAIRGROUNDS
BOX SEAT
$6.50 Tax Exempt
No Refund
105
SATURDAY JUNE 17
BIG BROTHER & THE HOLDING CO.
That Saturday, the air was still a little cool on the Monterey County Fairgrounds, near the ocean, like it often was that time of year.
"But that day, honey..."
"...that day..."
"... you set their hearts and blood on fire like nobody could have ever imagined possible."

COCKTAILS
MY GOD, JANIS, THAT WAS... UNBELIEVABLE! WHAT A SHOW! YOU WERE ALL IN TOP FORM!
YEAH, IT WAS A GAS, RIGHT, DONN? HA HA HA, WE REALLY ROCKED OUT, MAN!!
CAN YOU BELIEVE HOW FAR I'VE COME SINCE MY NATIVE TEXAS? PORT ARTHUR... AND ALL THE CRAP I WENT THROUGH THERE...
WHAT I REALLY, REALLY, REGRET, JANIS IS THAT WE WEREN'T ABLE TO SHOOT... NOT A SINGLE IMAGE OF THE ENTIRE CONCERT. ZILCH!
I KNOW, DAMN IT... BUT YOU SAW HOW JULIUS KARPEN, OUR MANAGER, WAS AGAINST IT.
BUMMER, MAN.
YEP. AND TO THINK SAM ANDREW AND I WERE ON BOARD WITH YOU FILMING! BUT NOOOO, HE WAS DEAD SET AGAINST IT, DAMN IT! AND TO GET AROUND THAT...
THERE MIGHT BE SOMETHING WE COULD TRY, BUT...
...YOU MUST KNOW ALBERT GROSSMAN, RIGHT?
YEAH, OF COURSE.
100

JANIS! IT'S GREAT TO MEET YOU! I WAS... STUNNED! STUNNED! YOU HAVE A BRIGHT FUTURE AHEAD OF YOU, TRUST ME!
DOESN'T SHE, CLIVE? JANIS, THIS IS CLIVE DAVIS. THE NEW HEAD OF COLUMBIA RECORDS.
REALLY? YOU REALLY LIKED IT?! I'M SO HAPPY TO HEAR THAT!
JANIS, I'LL EVEN GO A STEP FURTHER THAN ALBERT, AND SAY THAT WE ABSOLUTELY *HAVE* TO WORK TOGETHER! THE SOONER THE BETTER!
THAT'S GROOVY, MAN! I CAN'T WAIT TO TELL THE OTHERS THAT CBS LIKES US!!
BUT THERE'S A SNAG, RIGHT, DONN? MY SHOW WITH BIG BROTHER WASN'T FILMED... SUCH A BUMMER...
OUR MANAGER WAS AGAINST IT.
SO WE THOUGHT, IF WE COULD GO ON AGAIN TOMORROW... WE MIGHT GET HIM TO SAY YES TO DONN'S FILM...
YOU THINK MAYBE YOU COULD BACK UP THAT REQUEST, ALBERT? PART OF MY BAND IS ALREADY ON BOARD, AND I'LL GET THE OTHERS, TOO.
HMMM... I'M NO MAGICIAN, BUT... I DO HAVE *SOME* INFLUENCE...
101

WOW! THAT WAS REALLY HEAVY!
"Even those who knew the business, like Cass Elliott from the Mamas & the Papas, couldn't believe what they were hearing..."
102

Music, Love and Fl
"And you were only twenty-four, hon..."
103

YYY YYYYEEEEEEEEEAAAAAAHHHHH
BRAVO
HOURRAAAH
YES YES
When you walked off stage, as giddy as a schoolgirl who was just handed her diploma...
...you weren't the only one who sensed just how pivotal that moment was...
There were other great acts that day, of course...
...but it had become clear to all present that the future of music would now have to contend with you, sweetheart.
After the festival, several magazines reporting on Monterey wrote that you had been the true queen of the party.
And it was true.

HIPPIES DRESS LIKE SAVAGES FROM BORNEO.
JAMES DIBBLE
A.B.C. NEWS
HAVE THE RELIGIOUS BEHAVIOR OF HINDUS.
Summer of Lo
THE MATING HABITS OF RABBITS.
THE DRUG RITUALS OF THE CHINESE.
SUMMER OF LOVE
THE AUSTRALIAN ABORIGINES' GRASP OF ECONOMICS.
AND THE KINDNESS OF THE ORIGINAL CHRISTIANS.
LOVE NOT WAR
PEACE
YOUTH PEACE WALK
END THE SLAUGHT IN VIET
BAN NAPALM
WE WAN PEAC NOW

Your brand new fame made you even more visible and desirable... At long last, you could quench your thirst for love! And you didn't exactly hold back, sweetheart...
THAT WHOLE VIETNAM MESS IS ONLY GETTING WORSE...
MMH? OH, JOE, YOU'RE HOPELESS... FORGET ABOUT VIETNAM AND COME TAKE CARE OF ME, BABY...
our brand new fame made you even more visible and desirable... At long last, you coul
quench your thirst for love! And you didn't exactly hold back, baby...
I LOVE WHAT I FEEL WHEN I'M WITH YOU, JIMI! I'VE GOT THE SOUL OF A BLACK MAMA. I'VE ALWAYS KNOWN THAT.

I WOULD'VE DONE ANYTHING TO TALK TO YOU...
GET OUT, ERIC. WHY ME?! CREAM IS MUCH MORE FAMOUS THAN WE ARE!
I HATED YOU WHEN I FIRST MET YOU BACK IN THE SPRING IN SANTA MONICA, JIM MORRISON! BUT I ENDED UP GETTING YOU ANYWAY, MOTHERFUCKER. HA HA HA!
And, lastly, in the summer of '67, you eventually won over the one you'd been fascinated by for months... The beautiful Peggy Caserta. One of your most enduring love affairs.
107

But the magical parenthesis was about to close...

NOVEMBER 11, 1967. REMEMBER THIS DAY, PEOPLE!
THE CBS CONTRACT IS NOW OFFICIAL! THE WORLD IS WAITING FOR JANIS JOPLIN!
CBS
WHAT, WE DON'T COUNT?
From that moment, the worm was already in the apple...
BUT CAREFUL, DON'T FORGET THE RULES. HEROIN IS *STRICTLY* FORBIDDEN. I WILL BE INFLEXIBLE!
However, that wouldn't be obvious right away... And in the meantime, there was a lot of fun to be had...
ANDERSON
THEATRE
Janis Joplin

HOTEL
CHELSEA
BACK SO SOON?! IT'S NICE TO SEE YOU AGAIN, MISS JOPLIN! WELCOME!
I'M GLAD YOU SEEM TO BE ENJOYING MANHATTAN.
YEAH, HI, BARNEY. NICE TO SEE YOU AGAIN TOO. SAY, JUST BETWEEN US...
I HEAR THERE'S A CERTAIN KRISTOFFERSON HERE... MUSICIAN... REAL FOXY GUY...
I ONLY TAKE FOXY GUYS TO BED. IT'S A MATTER OF PRINCIPLE...
MISS JOPLIN, I... I'M SORRY, BUT WE'RE NOT ALLOWED TO GIVE OUT OUR GUESTS' ROOM NUMBERS, YOU KNOW THAT.
I'M DISAPPOINTED IN YOU, BARNEY. I THOUGHT YOU WERE COOL. AND I ASKED NICELY.
SLEEPING ALONE... I MEAN REALLY...
DING
GOING UP?
110

ARE YOU LOOKING FOR SOMEONE?
YES, I'M LOOKING FOR KRIS KRISTOFFERSON.

LITTLE LADY, YOU'RE IN LUCK, I AM KRIS KRISTOFFERSON.
OH YEAH? FUNNY, I THOUGHT YOU'D BE TALLER.

WHAT'S YOUR OTHER NAME?
COHEN. LEONARD COHEN. FROM MONTREAL. POET AND MUSICIAN.

HMPFF. YOU CAME HERE TO READ POETRY TO OLD LADIES, IN OTHER WORDS.

DING!
I'LL MAKE AN EXEMPTION TO MY FOXY RULE FOR YOU.
YOU'RE STAYING WITH ME TONIGHT, LEONARD FROM MONTREAL.
HOTEL CHELSEA

WHERE THE HELL IS SHE? WE HAVE AN ALBUM TO RECORD, DAMN IT!
ANOTHER ONE OF THOSE ENDLESS PHOTO SHOOTS... *LIFE, VOGUE, THE VILLAGE VOICE, THE NEW YORK TIMES...* EVER SINCE OUR SHOW AT THE ANDERSON THEATER, IT'S BEEN NON-STOP!

BUT IT'S JUST HER, HAVE YOU NOTICED? IT'S LIKE THE REST OF US ARE INVISIBLE.

YEP. SAME GOES FOR GROSSMAN. SHE'S ALL HE SEES!

BIG BROTHER AS A BACKUP BAND... SONOVABITCH...
AND I'M PRETTY SURE THE PRODUCER GUY THEY STUCK US WITH, THAT JOHN SIMON GUY, TAKES US FOR IDIOTS TOO...

IT'S TRUE, GUYS. THE PRESSURE IS ON, AND NOT JUST A LITTLE!
FINISHING THE RECORDING OF THIS SECOND ALBUM IS NOT GONNA BE A WALK IN THE PARK... WE JUST HAVE TO HANG IN THERE.

WHAT? WHAT THE HELL HAPPENED?! THIS WAS ALL SUPPOSED TO BE FOR FUN!
112

Summertime - ©George Gershwin, DuBose Heyward, Ira Gershwin. 1935.

WE SHOULD TRY SOMETHING MORE... FAR OUT...
SORRY, JOHN, BUT... NO. I DON'T THINK SO.
LET'S AT LEAST GIVE IT A SHOT AND SEE, OKAY?
IF YOU'RE ALL IN FAVOR, THEN FINE.
BUT COUNT ME OUT.
JANIS... WHAT'S THE HARM IN TRYING?
PLAYING IT AGAIN AND AGAIN, FASTER, LOUDER, TOUGHER? LISTEN...
I *KNOW* HOW THIS SONG SHOULD SOUND. PERIOD.
AND SO,
I'M SPLIT-TING.
114

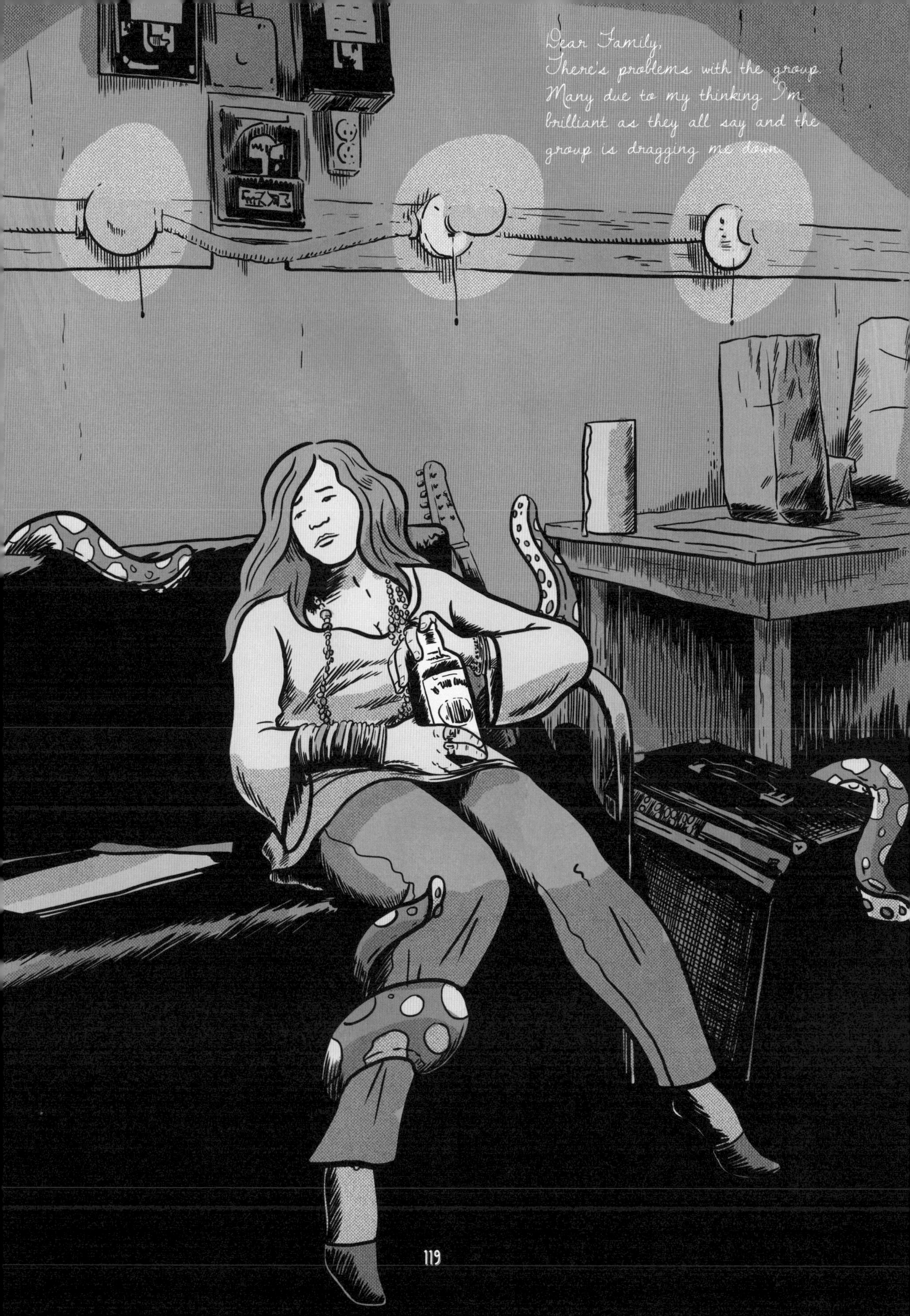
Dear Family,
There's problems with the group. Many due to my thinking I'm brilliant as they all say and the group is dragging me down.

WE ALL AGREE, CLIVE! WE WANT ROBERT CRUMB TO DO THE COVER!
HE'S FAR OUT! A HUGE STAR BACK ON THE WEST COAST...
UH-HUH... YOU SURE? WE HAVE SOME PRETTY GOOD ARTISTS IN OUR ART DEPARTMENT, YOU KNOW...
BUT NOBODY CAN DRAW DRUGGIN' OR SEXIN' LIKE HE CAN, HA HA HA!
ROBERT ALREADY SHOWED US HIS SKETCHES, YOU'LL SEE, THEY'RE OUTTA SIGHT! AND VERY ORIGINAL!
FINE. WHERE ARE WE ON THE TITLE?
WE WERE THINKING SOMETHING WITH A HOOK, LIKE *DOPE, SEX AND CHEAP THRILLS*...
OH NO, JANIS, ABSOLUTELY NOT!! THERE *ARE* LIMITS, YOU KNOW! I'LL LET *CHEAP THRILLS* SLIDE, EVEN THOUGH I FIND IT...
BUT *DOPE AND SEX*... GOOD LORD! WE'LL HAVE THE DISTRIBUTORS, THE AUDIENCE, THE MORALITY GROUPS AND GOD KNOWS WHO ELSE ON OUR BACK! NO, NO AND NO! AND THAT'S FINAL!
The No. 1 album in the country.
(And a gold one, too.)
CHEAP THRILLS
BIG BROTHER & THE HOLDING COMPANY
Maybe your boss wasn't entirely wrong that day, gorgeous...
Although... Once the album came out, nothing or nobody was able to control anything... One million copies sold in the first month alone, babe. It was unheard of.

I REALIZE IT'S A PARADOX, JANIS: *CHEAP TRILLS* IS A HUGE HIT AND THE AUDIENCE LOVES YOU, BUT... WE CAN'T GO ON LIKE THIS...
EVEN THE *LOS ANGELES FREE PRESS* IS DISTANCING ITSELF FROM THE BAND. THAT'S SAYING A LOT...
DEGREFF COLOURS
ROLLING STONE, VARIETY, CREEM AND THEN SOME: EVEN THE POSITIVE REVIEWS, AND THERE ARE A LOT, SAY THAT BIG BROTHER ISN'T GOOD ENOUGH FOR YOU.
I KNOW THIS ISN'T A SURPRISE, WE ALREADY BROUGHT IT UP WHEN RECORDING THE ALBUM.
BUT THIS TIME IT'S URGENT.
BEFORE THE WEEK'S OVER, WE'RE ISSUING A PRESS RELEASE ANNOUNCING YOUR SPLIT FROM BIG BROTHER AND THE HOLDING COMPANY. WE NEED TO CUT THE CHORD!
FINE, BUT DO IT NOW! I'M GIVING YOU 48 HOURS TOPS.
I... HOW DO... WAIT, UM... LET ME... LET ME TALK TO THEM FIRST, OK? PLEASE?
117

HOTEL CHELSEA
TALK ABOUT BETRAYAL!! WHO THE HELL FOUNDED THIS BAND, HUH?! WHERE WOULD SHE EVEN BE TODAY WITHOUT US?...
AND SHE JUST TELLS US IN HER ROOM, LIKE A PRINCESS HOLDING AN AUDIENCE...
LISTEN, I RATHER AGREE... THAT WAS HARSH... BUT BETTER JUST ACCEPT IT AND MOVE ON, NO?
HOTEL
CHELSEA
WE STILL HAVE LOTS OF MUSICAL PROSPECTS... WE HAVE A BAND AND A NAME WE CAN FIND ANOTHER LEAD VOCALIST.
THE FABULOUS FURRY FREAK BROTHERS
SAM? I ALSO WANTED TO SAY...
YES?
LISTEN, I... I DIDN'T WANT TO TELL YOU IN FRONT OF THE OTHERS, IT'S EMBARRASSING ENOUGH AS IT IS, BUT...
I'M GOING TO NEED SOMEONE LIKE YOU FOR THE NEXT CHAPTER, AND... NO MATTER WHO THE NEW MUSICIANS ARE...
...I WOULD LOVE IT IF YOU STAYED WITH THE BAND...
118

HEY, STANLEY!
WHAT'S SHAKING, MAN? LET ME GUESS, YOU WERE SENT TO COVER THE CONCERT BY... *BILLBOARD? ESQUIRE?*
ROLLING STONE. THEY WANT A PIECE ON JOPLIN AND HER NEW BAND, THE KOZMIC BLUES BAND. THEY'RE PRETTY MUCH THE ONLY WHITE BAND IN THE STAX LINEUP.
AND WHAT DO YOU THINK OF THESE WHITE GUYS?
IT'S NOT SO MUCH THAT THEY'RE WHITE, BUT THAT THEY JUST GOT HIRED. NOT SURE THEY'RE READY, EVEN WITH MIKE BLOOMFIELD TO GET THEM THERE...
I KNOW SAM ANDREW A LITTLE. HE'S THE ONLY ONE FROM BIG BROTHER WHO STAYED WITH JANIS. HE SAYS THAT TECHNICALLY, THEY'RE GOOD, BUT THAT... THEY'RE BASICALLY EMPLOYEES. THE FIRE IS GONE.
LOOKS LIKE YOU GOT THE SKINNY ON THEM.
YEAH BABY!
EITHER WAY, THE EVENING'S GONNA BE A GAS, MAN! ALBERT KING, BOOKER T AND THE MG'S, CARL AND RUFUS THOMAS... ALL THE STAX BIG SHOTS ARE PLAYING TOMORROW!
STAX
SOULSVILLE
U. S. A.
119

PLEASE WELCOME IN MEMPHIS
FOR THIS STAXS CHRISTMAS CONCERT
JANIS JOPLIN AND THE KOZMIC BLUES BAND
NOT A SINGLE ENCORE... SHOW OVER AFTER THREE NUMBERS.
YEAH... KIND OF A MIXED REACTION, HUH?
DISASTROUS, YOU MEAN. I ALREADY HAVE MY HOOK: *JOPLIN DIES IN MEMPHIS.*
120

CHAPTER 4

Lost and Distraught

AS YOU MAY KNOW, I'M SINGING WITH A NEW BAND NOW...

THIS MEANS NEW STUFF, SO WE'RE GONNA PLAY SOME JAZZ TO WAKE YOU UP.

Despite the Memphis disaster, you seemed to rebound just fine, daughter...

But your karma had changed so much...

HOLY FUCKING SHIT, SHE'S BARELY BREATHING!
OH MY GOD, SHE'S GONNA DIE, SHE'S GONNA DIE, SHE'S--
JANIS, JANIS, COME BACK, BABY... COME BACK!
FARBENFABRIKEN FRIED R. BAYER & C° ELBERFELD.
Heroin
SUNSHINE, GET ME A BASIN OF COLD WATER AND ICE CUBES... NOW!!
AND LOTS OF SALT DISSOLVED IN THE WATER. HURRY!
HOLY CRAP, SHE'S DRENCHED IN SWEAT... A ND HER PULSE IS RACING...
THERE, OKAY, SHE SWALLOWED... JANIS... JANIS! YES, THAT'S RIGHT, JUST A LITTLE MORE...
LOUARK!
OKAY. PHEW. WE DID IT. SHE'S COMING TO.
MAN *ALIVE!* THAT WAS A CLOSE ONE!!
HELP... IT HURTS...

In the spring, Europe was the perfect change of scenery for you, honey...
LONDON
AMSTERDAM
FRANKFURT
PARIS
The Europeans loved you from the get-go, even those who had never heard of you before...
124

STOCKHOLM
ENHAVN
And over there, perhaps due to long distance bonding, the Kozmic Blues Band finally started to sound like a real band.
125

And so after Europe, it was time for the media. Your notoriety knew no bounds...

You alone were in the spotlight now.

Of all the TV hosts you met on your rise to fame, this one was your favorite...

NOT BAD!

WELL HERE WE ARE, TOGETHER AGAIN AT LAST.

There was an almost instant chemistry between you two....

MAY I LIGHT YOUR FIRE, MY CHILD?

GUESS NOT, NO...

CLIC CLIC CLIC

APPARENTLY NOT... WELL, I WOULD HAVE BET AGAINST IT MYSELF...

...maybe even more...
I SAW YOU AT THE FILLMORE AND A FEW OTHER PLACES, AND IT'S REALLY AN... ECSTATIC EFFECT THAT YOU HAVE.

He himself, later in life, discreetly and elegantly hinted at it with calculated ambiguity...
WE WERE CLOSE FRIENDS. AND, I'LL BE FRANK WITH YOU, WE MAY HAVE BEEN INTI-MATE... OR NOT... MY MEMORY ISN'T WHAT IT USED TO BE...

126

But that man's real talent was the way he spontaneously understood who you truly were. And how he got you to talk about what you loved...
DO YOU READ MUCH?
QUIETLY BY THE FIRE, REREADING DICKENS?
YES, ON THE PLANE.
THAT'S NOT MY STYLE, REALLY, HA HA HA!

HAVE YOU EVER HAD A DESIRE TO JUST LEAVE THE STAGE, AND SAY, I'M SORRY, IT ISN'T WORKING TONIGHT FOLKS?
THE STAGE IS THE BEST THING THAT'S EVER HAPPENED TO ME!

WHAT ABOUT GROUPIES? I WONDER IF YOU LADY ROCK STARS HAVE MALE GROUPIES?
NOT NEARLY ENOUGH, NO, HA HA HA!

...what you loved more than anything.
WHEN YOU WALK ON STAGE AND START PLAYING... IT'S NOT NECESSARILY ABOUT MISERY, OR HAPPINESS...
IT'S ABOUT LETTING YOURSELF FEEL ALL THOSE THINGS THAT YOU ALREADY HAVE ON THE INSIDE BUT THAT YOU TRY TO PUSH ASIDE BECAUSE THEY DON'T MAKE FOR POLITE CONVERSATION.

There would even be one last TV interview with you two, shot a year after that first one on ABC...

Who could have known it would be the last?

HOLY SHIT, SAM!!! CHECK IT OUT, MAN!
WOOD
WOW... THIS IS TOO MUCH, SAM... WE'VE NEVER HAD A CROWD LIKE THIS BEFORE... THIS IS BLOWING MY MIND!
DON'T PANIC... LOOK HOW THE PEOPLE FROM WOODSTOCK VENTURES WELCOME THEIR GUESTS...
WE HAVE ALL WE NEED TO WAIT FOR HOURS, IF NEED BE!
GOOD THING PEGGY'S HERE... I CAN HANDLE ANY DISASTER WITH HER AT MY SIDE! SHE ALWAYS HAS... WHAT IT TAKES TO CHEER ME UP, IF YOU KNOW WHAT I MEAN...
That was the problem with Peggy, sweetheart: even romantically, she was... toxic for you.

TOCK
And that day, The chaotic organization of the Woodstock Festival added to it plentifully...
JANIS, YOU'LL HAVE TO FORGIVE US,
BUT THE SCHEDULE IS ALL MESSED UP...
THIS MEANS YOU'RE NOT GOING ON A FOR A GOOD WHILE...
BUT AT LEAST YOU'RE ALL SET: THE BAR IS YOURS!
THERE YOU HAVE IT: ALL THE BEST REASONS IN THE WORLD TO GET DRUNK FOR CHEAP!
I'M GONNA NEED SOME UPPERS AFTER-WARDS!
WE SHOULD TELL JANIS SHE'S ON SOON, RIGHT? SHE LOOKS REALLY OUT OF IT...
YOU KNOW WHAT THEY SAY, SHE'S GOT A HIGH TOLERANCE FOR THAT STUFF... BUT YOU'RE RIGHT, SHE NEEDS TO GET READY.
129
133

And then finally, around two a.m., you had no choice but to go on stage, baby doll.
Honestly? It would be lying to say that was your best show, sweetheart... But on the other hand, that night...
HOW ARE YOU OUT THERE, ARE YOU OK?
...everyone could see, as if they had you all to themselves, just how sincerely kind and thoughtful you were...
Which they remembered, no doubt...
YOU'RE STONED, YOU GOT ENOUGH WATER, YOU GOT A PLACE TO SLEEP AND EVERYTHING?
As for the music...
Who really cared, deep down?
Everyone had come to realize that what was going on in that farmer's field that night went beyond the talent or inspiration of the moment...
Just being there meant being part of history forever.

AND YOU SAY YOU REALLY WANT TO QUIT?
WELL... I TRIED A DETOX CLINIC LAST SUMMER... COLD TURKEY FOR NINE DAYS, BUT IT DIDN'T WORK.
THAT'S WHY THEY SENT ME TO SEE YOU. YOU GET AMAZING RESULTS, THEY SAY. AND I THINK I REALLY NEED HELP...
...MMMHH...
MISS JOPLIN... HOW MANY TIMES HAVE YOU OVERDOSED?
UM... FIVE OR SIX...
LISTEN TO ME CAREFULLY... GIVEN YOUR LEVEL OF ADDICTION, THE PROCESS YOU SAY YOU WANT TO EMBARK ON IS... COMPLICATED. DIFFICULT. ARE YOU SURE YOU ARE TRULY MOTIVATED?

Greetings from
COPACABANA
HEY, HI THERE, GORGEOUS!
WHOA, HI FOXY! WAIT, LET ME GUESS: ARE YOU THE GIRL FROM IPANEMA, BY ANY CHANCE?
HA HA HA... NO... BETTER YET: I'M JANIS.
NICE TO MEET YOU, JANIS. I'M DAVID. WHY ARE YOU IN RIO, JANIS? FOR THE CARNIVAL? FOR VACATION?
FOR A CHANGE OF SCENERY. TRYING TO GET AWAY FROM SHOWBIZ... AND QUIT THE DOPE.
SHOWBIZ? DOPE?
THAT'S ONE THING I'M SURE I'LL LOVE ABOUT YOU, DAVID: YOU HAVE NO IDEA WHO I AM, DO YOU?

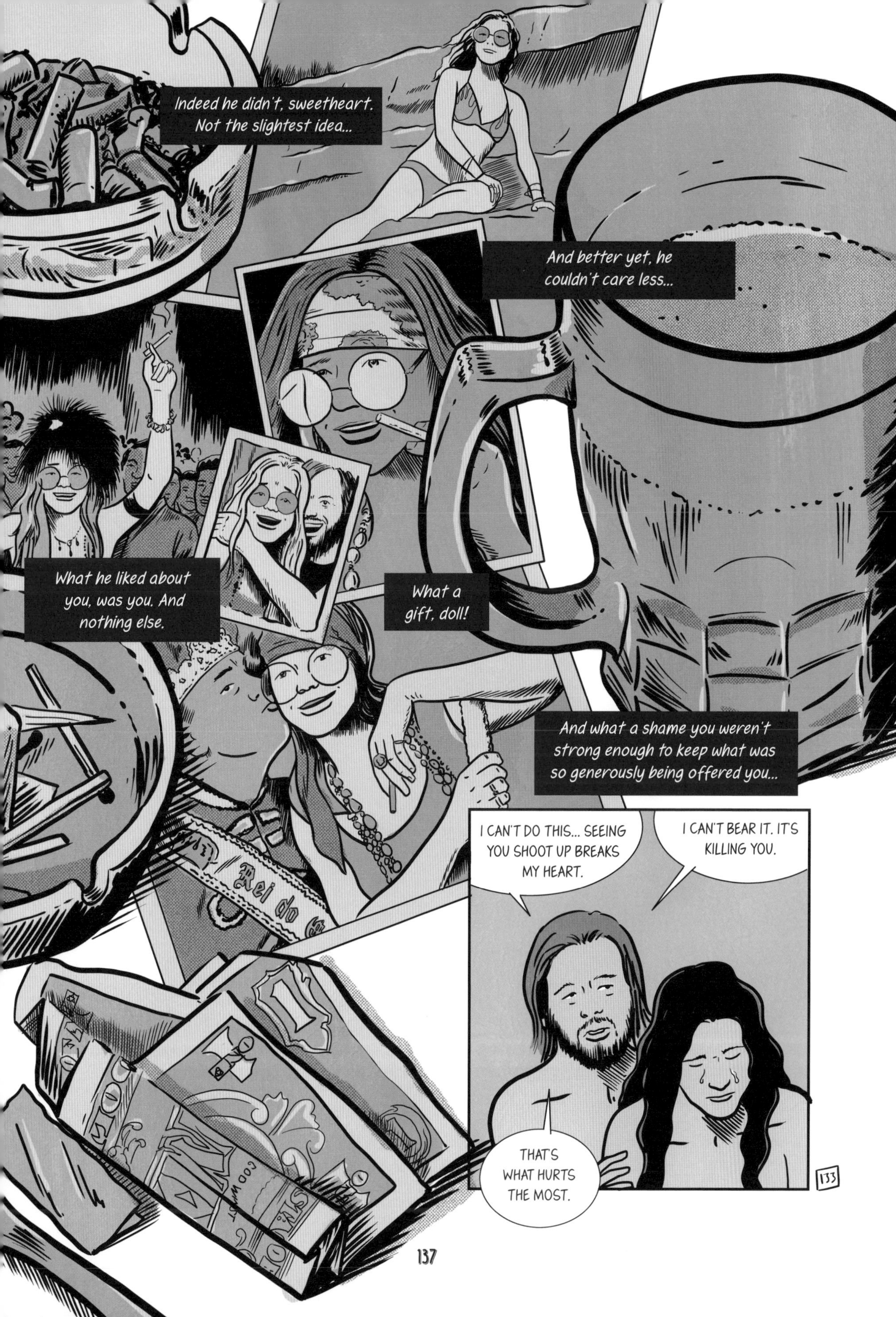
Indeed he didn't, sweetheart. Not the slightest idea...
And better yet, he couldn't care less...
What he liked about you, was you. And nothing else.
What a gift, doll!
And what a shame you weren't strong enough to keep what was so generously being offered you...
I CAN'T DO THIS... SEEING YOU SHOOT UP BREAKS MY HEART.
I CAN'T BEAR IT. IT'S KILLING YOU.
THAT'S WHAT HURTS THE MOST.
133

COME ON, JANIS, CAN'T YOU SEE HOW CRAZY IT ALL IS?
DAVID IN BRAZIL, SUNSHINE HERE, ALBERT AND MYRA IN NEW YORK... ONE BY ONE, YOU'VE ALIENATED ALL THOSE WHO CARE ABOUT YOU.

THE ONLY ONE LEFT IS PEGGY, AND YOU KNOW SHE'S NOT GOOD FOR YOU!
AND WHEN IT'S NOT HER... GOOD LORD, JANIS! LOOK AT ALL THOSE GUYS HOVERING AROUND HERE, SHOWING UP AT OUR PATHETIC PARTIES: PARASITES, DEALERS, LOSERS...
YOU SHOULD BE ENJOYING YOUR SUCCESS, AND THIS NEW HOUSE, AND YOUR BELOVED PETS, YOU SHOULD BE BUILDING YOUR FUTURE AND... EVEN THE DAMN KOZMIC BLUES BAND BROKE UP, FOR CRYING OUT LOUD!

ARE YOU DONE?
'CAUSE IF YOU DON'T LIKE IT HERE IN LARKS-PUR, LINDA, YOU CAN ALWAYS LEAVE.

OKAY THEN. MESSAGE RECEIVED. I'LL BE GONE TOMORROW.
134

YES, THAT'S IT! THAT'S IT EXACTLY!
YOU SEE, ALBERT, IT'S THE RIGHT COMBINATION! WE ONLY MET A FEW DAYS AGO AND WE ALREADY SOUND LIKE A REAL BAND!
YEAH, YOU'RE RIGHT. GREAT CASTING FROM MIKE BLOOMFIELD AND NICK GRAVENITES. WHAT ARE YOU GOING TO CALL YOURSELVES?
BOB NEUWIRTH HELPED ME FIND IT: FULL TILT BOOGIE! OKAY BOYS, HIT IT...
THE FULL TILT BOOGIE BAND
HOLD ON, I THINK I KNOW THAT SONG... DIDN'T ROGER MILLER ALREADY DO IT?
YEAH, MAN, HE DID... BUT WITH A COUNTRY SOUND. I'M DOING A MORE... UNIQUE VERSION, SEE.
IF THAT'S WHAT YOU WANT. WE NEED TO GET THE RIGHTS, THEN.
WELL, TALK ABOUT A STROKE OF LUCK, HA HA HA! THE SONGWRITER JUST MOVED IN A COUPLE OF DAYS AGO. ALBERT, MEET KRIS KRISTOFFERSON!
135

Hollywood wasn't the only reason he left, of course. Kris Kristofferson was an eligible bachelor and clearly, you weren't the first or the only woman on his dance card. But it was to you, and only you, that he gave Me and Bobby McGee.

FESTIVAL EXPRESS
FESTIVAL EXPRESS
That summer, you teamed up with quite a circus show... A traveling festival that took place during one week between Toronto and Calgary, aboard a train called the Festival Express 1970. Most of your musician friends were on board too, so needless to say, it was a good time...
On the train, Me and Bobby McGee practically became the official song of that traveling rock tour, the likes of which had never been seen before...
There were other shows after that, of course... Honolulu, New York, Port Chester, San Diego, San Rafael...
ME AND BOBBY McGEE
Whenever you could, you would do Me and Bobby McGee, and a few new songs from your upcoming album...
And then there was Boston. August 12, 1970. Nobody knew it at the time, of course, but that night was the last time anyone would ever again hear you sing in public.... It was your last concert, sweetheart.

WHY COME BACK TO PORT ARTHUR, MISS JOPLIN? AND WHY NOW?
BECAUSE IT'S MY TEN-YEAR HIGH SCHOOL REUNION.... EVEN THOUGH THOSE PEOPLE SURE AS HELL DIDN'T MAKE MY LIFE EASY!
WHAT DOES THIS REPRESENT FOR YOU? A PILGRIMAGE? PAYBACK?

HMM... NO COMMENT. I'LL LET YOU FIND THE RIGHT WORDS.

As you had so aptly written to your friend the painter Robert Rauschenberg: "We are the only two people to ever tear ourselves away from Port Arthur."
So why, then, after Boston, did you want to return to the scene of the crime?
Was it such a pressing need to feel loved, despite all the past humiliation?

Or did you still have so little confidence in yourself and in your music that you needed the approval of morons at all costs?
Port Arthur had never been very cheerful. Now your hometown struck you as down right gloomy.
138

Or was it an almost masochistic impulse to pour salt on your still open wounds in front of your former bullies?
I FELT... LEFT OUT.
AS A TEEN, I WAS TOLD TO "FIX" MYSELF, OR I WOULD END UP IN PRISON OR THE PSYCH WARD... AT 25, WHEN MY SECOND ALBUM CAME OUT, MY MOM SENT ME A TELEGRAM CONGRATULATING ME FOR NOT BEING IN JAIL...
DID YOUR FRIENDS BACK THEN MAKE YOU FEEL DIFFERENT?
JANIS !!
LAURA, MY KID SIS!! I DIDN'T KNOW YOU'D BE HERE.
DID YOU THINK I WOULD LET YOU LEAVE WITHOUT A HUG?
Not to mention your family, of course... More painful memories...
HOW ADORABLE! BUT I CAN'T STICK AROUND, HONEY... LOTS TO DO IN L.A.
OH, YOU'RE LEAVING SO SOON...
Love sure is messed up.
Why is it that only the love of total strangers matters, while the love of our family means nothing?
139

SUNSET SOUND
PAUL! PAUL! I THINK I'VE GOT IT!
CHECK IT OUT, PAUL, THIS IS HOW I SEE THE ALBUM COVER...
ON THE BACK, PICTURE A BAR COUNTER. I'M BEHIND THE BAR, SERVING FOUR DUDES WE ONLY SEE FROM BEHIND...
BUT ON THE FRONT SIDE, WE FLIP IT AROUND: I'M PICTURED FROM BEHIND, AND THE FOUR DUDES AT THE BAR ARE THE IDIOTS FROM FULL TILT BOOGIE, HA HA HA!!
BUT WAIT, THERE'S MORE!! INSIDE, ON THE SLEEVE, WE HAVE THIS WRITTEN IN BIG LETTERS...
DRINKS ARE ON PEARL
WELL, WHADDAYA THINK, ASSHOLES?
DRINKS ARE ON PEARL
140

NICE, FAR OUT, JANIS! BUT I'M NOT THE ONE YOU HAVE TO CONVINCE FOR THE COVER. THAT WOULD BE ALBERT AND CLIVE, IN NEW YORK.
I MEANT TO ASK: WHO STARTED CALLING YOU PEARL?

OH, THAT WAS DAVE RICHARDS! CUTE NICKNAME, NO?
I'LL SAY... IT'S A PERFECT MATCH FOR YOUR STYLE.

ALL RIGHT, BACK TO WORK, GUYS, WE GOT AN ALBUM TO FINISH!
YOU COMING, NICK? I WANT US TO WORK YOUR SONG IDEA, BURIED ALIVE IN THE BLUES...
I'LL BE RIGHT THERE. JUST NEED TO MAKE A CALL.

HI. NICK GRAVENITES FOR MYRA FRIEDMAN, PLEASE. THANKS.
NICK? GOOD TO HEAR FROM YOU. HOW ARE THINGS WITH JANIS IN L.A.?

LISTEN, MYRA, I... I'M NOT TOO SURE... SHE LOOKS OKAY, BUT... I HAVE A FEELING IT'S AN ACT...

SO YOU MEAN... YOU SHARE MY OMINOUS FEELING?
IT'S HARD TO BE SURE, BUT... SHE'S DRINKING LIKE A FISH, REFUSES TO TALK ABOUT IT, AND... SO YEAH, I AGREE WITH YOU, I'M AFRAID SHE'S BACK ON THE SMACK.

141

Such a paradox, baby doll...
On the outside, everything looked to be working out beautifully: a band that was finally in synch with your personality...
...and the most talented producer aroun
Paul Rothchild, to launch a musical projec
adapted to your expectations...
Even your boyfriend of the moment, Seth Morgan, seemed sensitive to your needs...
But of course, that was all a facade put on in a vain attempt to cover the gaping void of your existence...
And so, whenever she had the chance, Peggy Caserta, your evil genie, would return to haunt the corridors of your addiction...
Not to mention the countless dealers that swarmed about day and night at the Landmark Hotel, your home base whenever you were in L.A., drawn as they were to the artistic and bohemian clientele...
HOTEL
142

That's where you and Jim Morrison saw each other again...
...one last time.
HOTEL
MY OLD DRINKING PAL...
HAVE YOU HEARD? JIMI JUST DIED. IN LONDON. HIS LAST FIX KILLED HIM.
I CAME TO SAY GOODBYE. I'M LEAVING. QUITTING THE WHOLE RACKET. FOR GOOD. I'LL BE IN PARIS IN TWO DAYS. IF ALL GOES WELL, YOU'LL SEE MY NAME IN A LIBRARY CATALOGUE ONE OF THESE DAYS, AS AN AUTHOR. OR NOT.
143

HAPPY BIRTHDAY, JOHN!! HA HA HA HA!
COOL IDEA, SINGING FOR LENNON'S 30TH BIRTHDAY! I BET HE WON'T BE EXPECTING IT!
YEP, YOU CAN ALWAYS COUNT ON JANIS FOR THIS TYPE OF THING! THAT GIRL REALLY IS SWEET, MAN.
WELL BOYS, ARE YOU READY TO PARTY? HA HA HA!
WHERE TO, JANIS?
BARNEY'S BEANERY?
Barney's Beanery
GAMES & POOL
AGAIN?!! HECK, JANIS, WE'VE BEEN THERE EVERY NIGHT THIS WEEK!
Barney's Beanery
SO? DON'T YOU LIKE IT HERE?
HALF OF HOLLYWOOD AND ANYONE WHO MATTERS ON THE L.A. MUSIC SCENE STOPS BY HERE FOR A DRINK AT SOME POINT...
AND YOU EXPECT JANIS JOPLIN NOT TO BE HERE?
YOU'RE HOPELESS!

GUYS, TONIGHT IS A SPECIAL NIGHT... 'CAUSE WE'RE ALMOST DONE WITH THAT GODDAMNED ALBUM... AND 'CAUSE I'M SUPER JAZZED ABOUT THE GREAT WORK WE DID TOGETHER!
YOU SHOULD BE *JAZZED*, JANIS! PAUL KEEPS TELLING EVERYONE YOU'VE NEVER SUNG BETTER! AND FOR PAUL TO SAY NICE THINGS OUT LOUD...
NOW, WE REALLY NEED TO DISCUSS THE NEXT ALBUM...
WE CLOSE IN THIRTY MINUTES, PEOPLE. THIS IS LAST CALL!
Ding Ding
OH... I GUESS WE'LL DISCUSS IT TOMORROW.
OK, SO, DON'T FORGET: TOMORROW WE HAVE TO FINISH NICK'S *BURIED ALIVE IN THE BLUES.*
DAMN. GOOD THING I'M NOT SUPERSTITIOUS, HA HA HA. *BURIED ALIVE IN THE BLUES*... DAMN.
Barney's Beanery
145

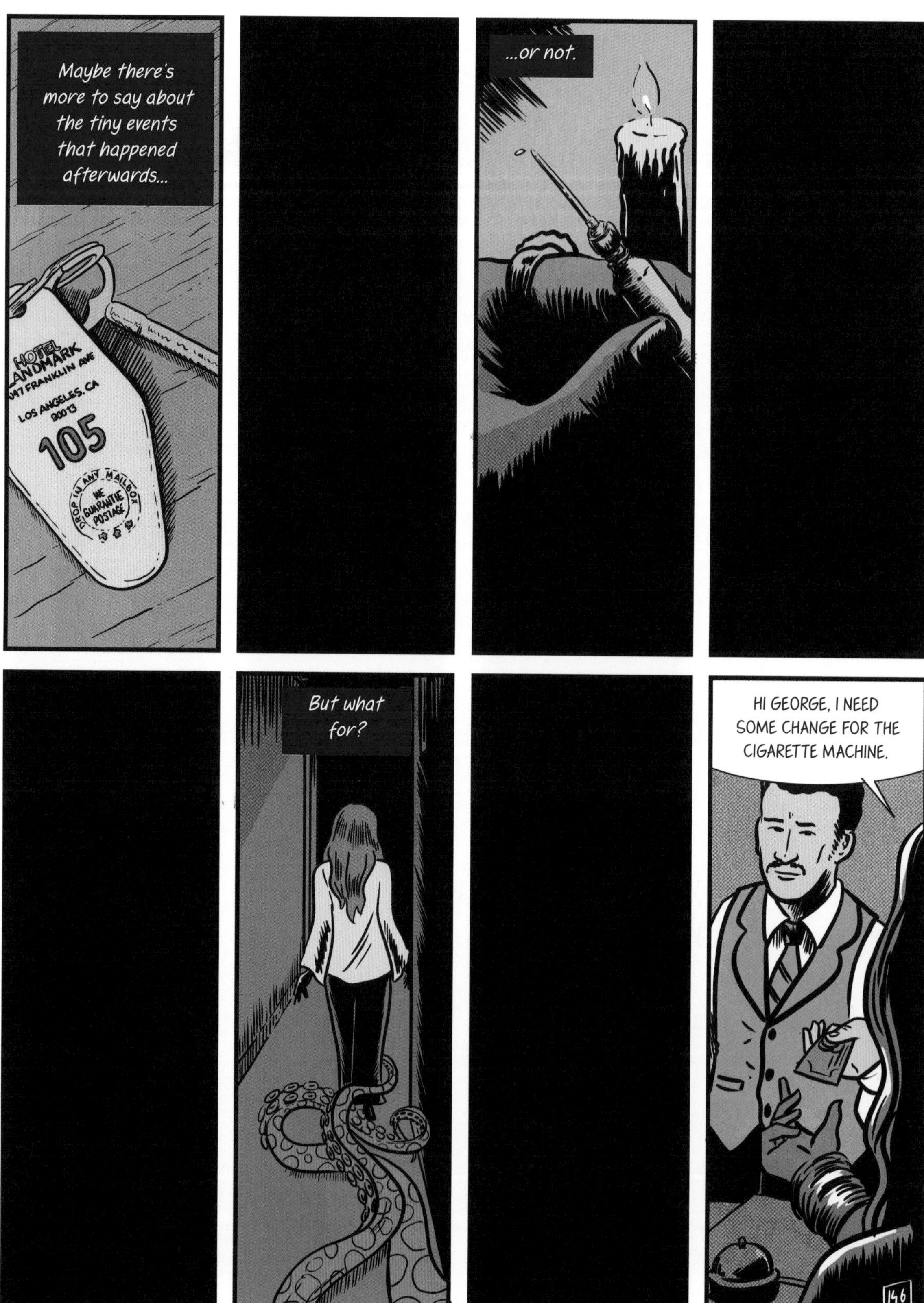
Maybe there's more to say about the tiny events that happened afterwards...
HOTEL LANDMARK
7047 FRANKLIN AVE
LOS ANGELES, CA
90013
105
DROP IN ANY MAILBOX
WE GUARANTEE POSTAGE
...or not.
But what for?
HI GEORGE, I NEED SOME CHANGE FOR THE CIGARETTE MACHINE.
146

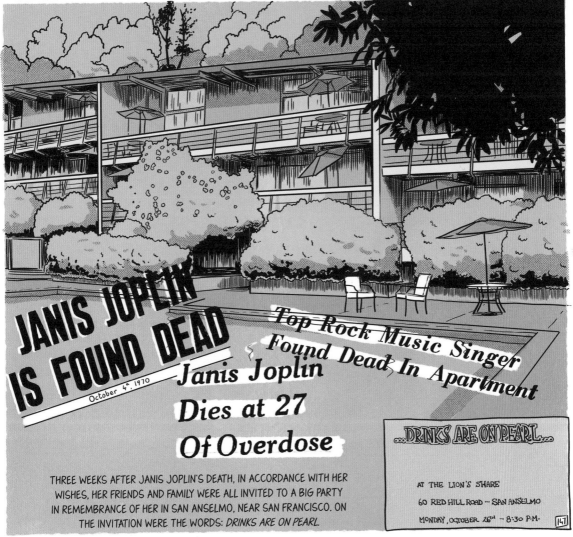

JANIS JOPLIN IS FOUND DEAD

October 4th, 1970

Top Rock Music Singer Found Dead In Apartment

Janis Joplin Dies at 27 Of Overdose

THREE WEEKS AFTER JANIS JOPLIN'S DEATH, IN ACCORDANCE WITH HER WISHES, HER FRIENDS AND FAMILY WERE ALL INVITED TO A BIG PARTY IN REMEMBRANCE OF HER IN SAN ANSELMO, NEAR SAN FRANCISCO. ON THE INVITATION WERE THE WORDS: *DRINKS ARE ON PEARL.*

...DRINKS ARE ON PEARL...

AT THE LION'S SHARE

60 RED HILL ROAD ... SAN ANSELMO

MONDAY, OCTOBER 26TH ~ 8:30 P.M.

147

Barely had you arrived in this world that you had to leave it, sweetheart... Too precocious, too uncompromising, too talented.

The first one to dare to become a superstar in the face of so much adversity...

For each of us, that is now your eternal legacy.

©Christopher 29/06/2020

148

CHARACTER GALLERY

(in order of appearance)

ELISABETH « BESSIE » SMITH (APRIL 15, 1894 – SEPTEMBER 26, 1937)

BESSIE SMITH WAS BORN IN TENNESSEE, WHERE SHE LEARNED SINGING AT A YOUNG AGE IN THE STREETS OF CHATTANOOGA, THEN LATER IN THE TRAVELING SHOW OF "MA" RAINEY. SHE IS CONSIDERED ONE OF THE GREATEST AMERICAN SINGERS OF THE TWENTIETH CENTURY, AND IN FACT WAS CALLED THE EMPRESS OF THE BLUES. SHE RECORDED OVER 120 SONGS, PRIMARILY AT COLUMBIA RECORDS.

ODETTA HOLMES (DECEMBER 31, 1930 – DECEMBER 2, 2008)

BORN IN BIRMINGHAM, ALABAMA, AND CHOOSING TO BE KNOWN ONLY BY HER FIRST NAME, ODETTA EMERGED ON THE U.S. MUSIC STAGE IN THE 1950S. WHILE HER MUSIC WAS MORE FOLK, IT ALSO DREW HEAVILY FROM THE BLUES. SHE WAS ALSO AN ACTIVIST IN THE CIVIL RIGHTS MOVEMENT.

GERTRUDE « MA » RAINEY (APRIL 26, 1886 – DECEMBER 22, 1939)

BORN IN GEORGIA, MA RAINEY IS ONE OF THE EARLY BLUES FIGURES, HENCE HER NICKNAME AS THE MOTHER OF THE BLUES. SHE INITIALLY PERFORMED AS PART OF MINSTREL AND VARIETY TRAVELING SHOWS BEFORE LATER RECORDING SOME ONE HUNDRED SONGS, MOST NOTABLY WITH PARAMOUNT RECORDS IN THE 1920S.

ELEANORA HARRIS FAGAN, ALIAS BILLIE HOLIDAY
(APRIL 7, 1915 – JULY 17, 1959)

BILLIE HOLIDAY WAS BORN IN PHILADELPHIA, BUT LIVED IN NEW YORK STARTING IN THE LATE 20S. SHE FIRST MADE A NAME FOR HERSELF ON THE CLUB CIRCUIT AT THE START OF THE FOLLOWING DECADE, WHERE SHE PERFORMED FOR LITTLE MONEY BEFORE SHE WAS DISCOVERED. CELEBRATED AND MUCH ADMIRED, SHE WENT ON TO BECOME ONE OF THE GREATEST JAZZ SINGERS OF THE CENTURY.

JIM LANGDON (1940 –)

JIM LANGDON WAS PART OF JOPLIN'S SMALL, TIGHT-KNIT GROUP OF FRIENDS GROWING UP IN PORT ARTHUR, WHO ALL SHARED A LOVED FOR CULTURE AND THE ARTS, AND HE CONTRIBUTED SIGNIFICANTLY TO HER BLOSSOMING INTO AN ARTIST. LATER, AS A REPORTER WITH THE *AUSTIN STATESMAN*, WHERE, AMONG OTHERS, HE WROTE A MUSIC COLUMN TITLED "NIGHT BEAT," HE ENCOURAGED HER TO RETURN TO MUSIC AFTER SHE HAD PRACTICALLY GIVEN UP SINGING FOLLOWING A FIRST AND DISASTROUS PERIOD IN SAN FRANCISCO.

GILBERT SHELTON (MAY 31, 1940 –)

BORN IN HOUSTON, GILBERT SHELTON WAS ONE OF THE GREAT MASTERS OF ALTERNATIVE AMERICAN COMICS. HE BEGAN PLYING HIS TRADE IN THE EARLY 1960S IN STUDENT NEWSPAPERS IN HOUSTON AND AUSTIN, THEN IN 1968 BECAME ONE OF THE CO-FOUNDERS OF THE RIP OFF PRESS PUBLISHING COLLECTIVE IN SAN FRANCISCO. THERE, HE CREATED THE SERIES THAT MADE HIM FAMOUS, THE FABULOUS FURRY FREAK BROTHERS. SHELTON WAS ONE OF JANIS JOPLIN'S MUSIC BUDDIES IN AUSTIN, IN THE EARLY DAYS OF HER ARTISTIC JOURNEY. HE HAS LIVED IN FRANCE FOR MANY YEARS. .

JACK « JAXON » JACKSON (MAY 15, 1941 - JUNE 8, 2006)

A TEXAN JUST LIKE JANIS JOPLIN WAS, JACK JACKSON WAS AN AUTHOR AND COMIC BOOK PUBLISHER WHO PLAYED A KEY ROLE IN THE GROWTH OF UNDERGROUND COMICS IN THE U.S. STARTING IN THE MID-1960S. AMONG OTHER THINGS, IN 1969 HE WAS ONE OF THE CO-FOUNDERS, ALONG WITH GILBERT SHELTON, DAVE MORIATY AND FRED TODD, OF THE RIP OFF PRESS PUBLISHING COLLECTIVE IN SAN FRANCISCO, WHICH, MOST NOTABLY, PUBLISHED GILBERT SHELTON'S COMICS.

POWELL ST. JOHN (SEPTEMBER 18, 1940 -)

BORN IN HOUSTON, POWELL ST. JOHN CROSSED PATHS WITH JANIS JOPLIN IN HER EARLY DAYS IN AUSTIN, WHERE, ALONG WITH LANNIE WIGGINS, THEY FORMED THE SHORT-LIVED TRIO CALLED THE WALLER CREEK BOYS. HE WENT ON TO COMPOSE A HALF-DOZEN SONGS FOR THE BAND 13TH FLOOR ELEVATORS, AND THEN TO MAKE A NAME FOR HIMSELF IN CALIFORNIA AS PART OF ANOTHER BAND, MOTHER EARTH.

KENNETH THREADGILL (SEPTEMBER 18, 1909 - MARCH 20, 1987)

A TEXAN BORN AND RAISED, KENNETH THREADGILL OPENED HIS FIRST BAR, THREADGILL'S TAVERN, IN AUSTIN AT THE END OF PROHIBITION. MANY MUSICIANS PERFORMED THERE AND ON OCCASION, HE WOULD SING ON STAGE HIMSELF. HE WAS ONE OF THE FIRST TO GIVE JANIS JOPLIN A SHOT AS A SINGER. SHE WAS ETERNALLY GRATEFUL FOR THAT AND FOR THE REST OF HER SHORT LIFE MAINTAINED A FRIENDSHIP WITH THREADGILL AND HIS WIFE MILDRED, EVEN INTERRUPTING A SUCCESSFUL HAWAIIAN TOUR IN 1970 TO FLY BACK TO AUSTIN JUST TO SING AT HER FRIEND KENNETH'S BIRTHDAY PARTY.

CHESTER LEO « CHET » HELMS (AUGUST 2, 1942 - JUNE 25, 2005)

OFTEN REFERRED TO AS ONE OF THE PEOPLE WHO DISCOVERED JANIS JOPLIN, THE CALIFORNIA-BORN "CHET" HELMS WAS ONE OF THE MAIN FIGURES BEHIND THE RISE OF COUNTERCULTURE IN SAN FRANCISCO IN THE MID-1960S. A BAND MANAGER AND CONCERT PROMOTER (THE FIRST PSYCHEDELIC LIGHT SHOWS), MOST NOTABLY AT THE MYTHICAL AVALON BALLROOM, WHERE HE WAS IN CHARGE OF THE PROGRAMMING, HE WAS CONSIDERED, ALONG WITH HIS RIVAL BILL GRAHAM, THE FATHER OF THE SUMMER OF LOVE.

DAVID FREIBERG (AUGUST 24, 1938 -)

BORN IN CINCINNATI, OHIO, DAVID FREIBERG, A VOCALIST AND MULTI-INSTRUMENTALIST (THOUGH BASS GUITAR REMAINED HIS INSTRUMENT OF CHOICE) WAS ONE OF THE FOUNDERS OF THE CALIFORNIAN BAND QUICKSILVER MESSENGER SERVICE, WHICH WAS A BIG HIT IN THE EARLY 1970S. HE WAS CLOSE TO JEFFERSON AIRPLANE AND JOINED SOME OF THE BAND MEMBERS IN THEIR NEW INCARNATION, JEFFERSON STARSHIP, WHEN IT LAUNCHED IN 1974.

PAT « SUNSHINE » NICHOLS (1949 -)

PAT NICHOLS, A MIXED-RACE NATIVE AMERICAN NICKNAMED SUNSHINE (ONE OF THE STREET NAMES FOR LSD) WAS A WAITRESS AT LEO SIEGLER'S COFFEE GALLERY WHEN SHE MET JANIS JOPLIN, AFTER WHICH THE TWO WOMEN BECAME GOOD FRIENDS. IN ADDITION TO DOING DRUGS, WHICH BROUGHT THEM TOGETHER, SUNSHINE, LINDA GRAVENITES AND JANIS JOPLIN MADE UP AN INFORMAL GROUP OF FRIENDS ALL BORN UNDER THE SIGN OF CAPRICORN, WHO CALLED THEMSELVES THE CAPRICORN LADIES. BOTH WOMEN WERE SEVERELY ADDICTED TO HEROIN AND MADE A PACT WITH EACH OTHER IN 1969: NOT TO SEE EACH OTHER AGAIN UNTIL THEY WERE CLEAN. THE CAPRICORN LADIES WERE PLANNING A REUNION TO THAT EFFECT ON OCTOBER 6, 1970 IN LOS ANGELES. JANIS JOPLIN DIED THE MORNING OF THE FOURTH.

PEGGY CASERTA (1941 -)

PEGGY CASERTA WAS BORN IN LOUISIANA AND MOVED TO SAN FRANCISCO IN THE 60S, WHERE SHE OPENED A FASHION BOUTIQUE CALLED MNASIDIKA IN THE HEART OF THE FAMED HAIGHT-ASHBURY HIPPIE NEIGHBORHOOD. AMONG HER REGULAR CLIENTELE WERE MEMBERS OF THE GRATEFUL DEAD AND OF BIG BROTHER AND THE HOLDING COMPANY. IT WAS UNDER THESE CIRCUMSTANCES THAT SHE BECAME ONE OF JANIS JOPLIN'S REGULAR LOVERS. A HEROIN ADDICT FOR DECADES, SHE WAS OFTEN ACCUSED OF BEING THE ROCK STAR'S EVIL GENIE. THE SCANDALOUS TELL-ALL MEMOIR SHE WROTE IN 1973, *GOING DOWN WITH JANIS*, DID NOT HELP IMPROVE THAT IMAGE. SHE RECENTLY DENIED SOME OF THE CLAIMS IN A SECOND BOOK, *I RAN INTO SOME TROUBLE (2018).*

JORMA KAUKONEN (DECEMBER 23, 1940 -)

ORIGINALLY FROM WASHINGTON, D.C. AND A PASSIONATE BLUESMAN, JORMA KAUKONEN MADE A NAME FOR HIMSELF IN SAN FRANCISCO IN THE EARLY 60'S. A GIFTED GUITAR PLAYER, HE WAS ONE OF THE CO-FOUNDERS OF JEFFERSON AIRPLANE IN 1965, ALONG WITH PAUL KANTNER AND MARTY BALIN. IN 1979, HE AND FELLOW AIRPLANE BAND MEMBER BASS PLAYER JACK CASADY FOUNDED A NEW BAND CALLED HOT TUNA, WHICH WAS A HIT WITH AUDIENCES THROUGHOUT THE 70S.

DAVID CROSBY (AUGUST 14, 1941 -)

A NATIVE OF LOS ANGELES, DAVID CROSBY EMBARKED ON HIS MUSICAL CAREER IN THE 1960S, NAMELY BY CO-FOUNDING, ALONG WITH ROGER MCGUINN, THE HIGHLY SUCCESSFUL BAND THE BYRDS IN 1964. IN 1969, HE BECAME ONE OF THE FOUNDERS OF CROSBY, STILLS & NASH, A BAND SOON TO BE JOINED BY NEIL YOUNG. THEIR CAREER TOGETHER WAS A SHORT BUT TRIUMPHANT ONE, WITH A SIGNIFICANT NUMBER OF ALBUMS SOLD AND A MEMORABLE PERFORMANCE AT WOODSTOCK. THE BAND WENT ON TO PERIODICALLY REUNITE TO PERFORM AND TOUR IN VARIOUS LINEUPS, WITH OR WITHOUT YOUNG.

MICHAEL BERNARD « MIKE » BLOOMFIELD (JULY 28, 1943 - FEBRUARY 15, 1981)

BORN IN CHICAGO AND DRAWN TO MUSIC, ESPECIALLY THE BLUES, AT AN EARLY AGE, MIKE BLOOMFIELD BECAME KNOWN IN THE MID-60S THROUGH HIS STUDIO WORK WITH BOB DYLAN AND, ESPECIALLY, AS ONE OF THE TWO REGULAR GUITARISTS (THE OTHER BEING ELVIN BISHOP) OF THE PAUL BUTTERFIELD BLUES BAND. IN 1967, HE LEFT THE BAND TO FORM THE ELECTRIC FLAG WITH NICK GRAVENITES. FOLLOWING THAT PERIOD, HE WORKED WITH MUSICIANS SUCH AS AL KOOPER AND STEPHEN STILLS, BUT DIDN'T MEET WITH COMMERCIAL SUCCESS. HIS SUDDEN DEATH IN THE EARLY 1980S WAS ATTRIBUTED TO AN OVERDOSE.

13TH FLOOR ELEVATORS (1966 - 1968)

A PIONEERING AMERICAN BAND IN THE ROCK GARAGE AND PSYCHEDELIC GENRES, 13TH FLOOR ELEVATORS WAS FOUNDED IN AUSTIN, TEXAS, IN 1966. EXTREMELY DRAWN TO SYNTHETIC DRUGS AND THE TRANSCENDENCE THEY PROMISED, THE BAND DIDN'T SURVIVE THE ADDICTION OF SEVERAL MEMBERS AND DISSOLVED IN 1968. A HANDFUL OF INSPIRED ALBUMS REMAIN A TESTAMENT TO THEIR UNIQUE MUSICAL JOURNEY.

TRAVIS RIVERS

TRAVIS RIVERS' CLAIM TO FAME IS TO HAVE CONVINCED JANIS JOPLIN, AT THE INSTIGATION OF CHET HELMS, TO RETURN TO SAN FRANCISCO AFTER HER DISASTROUS, DEPRAVED, AND ADDICTION-FUELED FIRST STAY THERE. IN JEST, JOPLIN LATER PAINTED HIM, IN A NOW FAMOUS RADIO INTERVIEW, AS AN AMAZING "LOVER" (SHE USED AN ALTOGETHER DIFFERENT TERM)--A FLATTERING BUT DOUBTLESS EXAGGERATED DESCRIPTION THAT STUCK WITH HIM FOR THE REST OF HIS LIFE. RIVERS ALSO WORKED AS A MUSIC MANAGER AND PRODUCER, NAMELY IN NASHVILLE.

DAVID « DAVE » GETZ (JANUARY 24, 1940 -)

DAVE GETZ WAS BORN IN BROOKLYN, STARTED PLAYING THE DRUMS AT THE AGE OF 14 AND ALSO STUDIED PAINTING. HE MOVED TO SAN FRANCISCO IN THE MID-60S AND BECAME INVOLVED IN THE MUSIC SCENE THERE. IN THE SPRING OF '66, HE JOINED BIG BROTHER AND THE HOLDING COMPANY, THREE MONTHS BEFORE JANIS JOPLIN RETURNED TO FRISCO AND ALSO JOINED THE BAND, WHICH MARKED THE BEGINNING OF THE EXTRAORDINARY MUSICAL JOURNEY ON WHICH THEY ALL EMBARKED TOGETHER.

JAMES MARTIN GURLEY (DECEMBER 22, 1939 - DECEMBER 20, 2009)

ORIGINALLY FROM DETROIT, A FAN OF JOHN COLTRANE AND OF BLUESMAN LIGHTNIN' HOPKINS, GUITARIST JAMES GURLEY MOVED TO SAN FRANCISCO IN 1962 WITH HIS WIFE NANCY, WHO BECAME A GOOD FRIEND OF JANIS JOPLIN BEFORE DYING OF A DRUG OVERDOSE IN 1969. AT THE INSTIGATION OF CHET HELMS, HE JOINED BIG BROTHER AND THE HOLDING COMPANY IN 1965 AND BECAME ONE OF THE KEY ARCHITECTS OF THE CALIFORNIA PSYCHEDELIC ROCK SCENE.

SAM HOUSTON ANDREW III (DECEMBER 18, 1941 - FEBRUARY 12, 2015)

BORN IN CALIFORNIA, GUITARIST SAM ANDREW WAS PART OF THE EFFERVESCENT WEST COAST MUSIC SCENE FROM THE EARLY 60'S ON. ALONG WITH PETER ALBIN, HE WAS ONE OF THE FOUNDERS OF BIG BROTHER AND THE HOLDING COMPANY AND LATER UNOFFICIALLY BECAME THE BAND'S MUSICAL DIRECTOR. HE WAS ALSO THE ONLY MEMBER OF THE BAND'S ORIGINAL LINEUP TO FOLLOW JANIS JOPLIN WHEN SHE DECIDED--AT ALBERT GROSSMAN'S URGING--TO LEAVE AND SURROUND HERSELF WITH A NEW BAND, THE KOZMIC BLUES BAND.

PETER SCOTT ALBIN (JUNE 6, 1944 -)

BORN IN SAN FRANCISCO, PETER ALBIN WAS INITIALLY A GUITAR PLAYER, BUT WHEN HE MET SAM ANDREW THEN JAMES GURLEY, ALSO BOTH GUITARISTS, HE OPTED TO PLAY THE BASS, INSTEAD. HE ALSO SANG VOCALS FOR BIG BROTHER AND THE HOLDING COMPANY UNTIL JANIS JOPLIN JOINED THE BAND AND BECAME THE LEAD SINGER. WHEN THE BAND SPLIT UP IN 1969, HE BRIEFLY JOINED COUNTRY JOE AND THE FISH ALONG WITH DRUMMER DAVE GETZ, BEFORE REFORMING BIG BROTHER, FIRST WITH THE BAND'S ORIGINAL MEMBERS, THEN WITH OTHER MUSICIANS.

WILLIE MAE « BIG MAMA » THORNTON (DECEMBER 11, 1926 - JULY 25, 1984)

BORN IN MONTGOMERY, ALABAMA, BIG MAMA THORNTON WAS A PASTOR'S DAUGHTER WHO FIRST LEARNED MUSIC AT CHURCH. AFTER TOURING EXTENSIVELY THROUGH THE SOUTH FOR SEVERAL YEARS AS PART OF A TRAVELING MUSICAL REVUE, SHE RECORDED "HOUND DOG" IN 1953, WHICH CLIMBED UP THE RHYTHM & BLUES CHARTS AND WENT ON TO BECOME A ROCK & ROLL CLASSIC THANKS TO ELVIS PRESLEY'S VERSION OF IT. ANOTHER OF HER SONGS, "BALL AND CHAIN," WOULD BE MADE FAMOUS THROUGH JANIS JOPLIN.

ROBERT « BOB » SHAD (FEBRUARY 12, 1920 - MARCH 13,1985)

BORN ABRAHAM SHADRINSKY, BOB SHAD BEGAN WORKING AS A MUSIC PRODUCER IN THE 1940S, MAINLY IN THE FIELDS OF JAZZ (SARAH VAUGHAN, MAX ROACH, CHARLIE PARKER) AND BLUES (BIG BILL BROONZY, LIGHTNIN' HOPKINS). IN 1964, HE FOUNDED THE MAINSTREAM LABEL, THE FIRST TO SIGN AND RECORD BIG BROTHER AND THE HOLDING COMPANY, IN 1967. HE WENT ON TO SPECIALIZE IN FUNK AND SOUL.

BILL GRAHAM (JANUARY 8, 1931 - OCTOBER 25, 1991)

BILL GRAHAM (BIRTH NAME: WOLODIA GRAJONCA) WAS BORN IN BERLIN, TO A JEWISH FAMILY ORIGINALLY FROM RUSSIA. FACING NAZI PERSECUTION, THEY FLED GERMANY, FIRST TO FRANCE AND THEN TO AMERICA, WHERE HE BECAME A U.S. CITIZEN. HE MOVED TO SAN FRANCISCO IN THE EARLY 60S AND BECAME A CONCERT PROMOTER. HIS TWO VENUES, THE FILLMORE AUDITORIUM AND THE WINTERLAND BALLROOM, WERE HUGELY SUCCESSFUL, MAKING HIM ONE OF THE GREAT PATRONS OF WEST COAST MUSIC AND, MORE GENERALLY, OF AMERICAN ROCK IN THAT ERA.

OTIS RAY REDDING (SEPTEMBER 9, 1941 - DECEMBER 10, 1967)

OTIS REDDING WAS BORN IN GEORGIA AND BEGAN MAKING A NAME FOR HIMSELF IN 1964. AN INCREDIBLY SKILLED SINGER AND PERFORMER, HE DAZZLED ALL THOSE WHO HAD THE GOOD FORTUNE OF SEEING HIM ON STAGE, LIKE JANIS JOPLIN, WHO DREW PART OF HER INSPIRATION FROM HIS VOCAL STYLE. HE DIED IN A PLANE CRASH AT THE THRESHOLD OF A CAREER THAT PROMISED TO BE EXCEPTIONAL.

LINDA ANNE GRAVENITES (DECEMBER 23, 1939 - 2002)

BORN LINDA ANNE MCCLEAN IN NEW YORK, AND DRAWN EARLY ON TO THE EFFERVESCENCE OF CALIFORNIA, WHERE SHE MET AND MARRIED MUSICIAN NICK GRAVENITES, FROM WHOM SHE WOULD QUICKLY SEPARATE, LINDA GRAVENITES WAS ONE OF JANIS JOPLIN'S CLOSEST FRIENDS FOR YEARS. SHE WAS HER ROOMMATE IN VARIOUS APARTMENTS AND HOUSES, AND OFTEN SERVED AS HER STYLE GURU, HELPING THE SINGER BUILD A WARDROBE AND A LOOK, WHICH, OVER THE YEARS, BECAME ONE OF THE KEY COMPONENTS OF HER IDENTITY AS AN ARTIST.

ALBERT BERNARD GROSSMAN (MAY 21, 1926 - JANUARY 25, 1986)

BORN IN CHICAGO TO A JEWISH FAMILY ORIGINALLY FROM RUSSIA, ALBERT GROSSMAN WAS THE ARCHETYPAL AMERICAN TALENT MANAGER, A SHREWD AND AGGRESSIVE BUSINESSMAN WHO WAS FIERCELY PROTECTIVE OF HIS ARTISTS. HIS IMPRESSIVE SKILLS AND HIS ROSTER OF CLIENTS HELPED FURTHER THE GROWTH OF FOLK MUSIC IN THE VERY EARLY 1960S, WITH MUSICIANS LIKE PETER, PAUL AND MARY AND BOB DYLAN. HE LATER WORKED WITH ARTISTS FROM BLUES AND ROCK, SUCH AS TODD RUNDGREN, RICHIE HAVENS, JOHN LEE HOOKER AND, OF COURSE, JANIS JOPLIN. ALBERT GROSSMAN DIED OF A HEART ATTACK ON BOARD THE CONCORDE FROM NEW YORK TO LONDON.

DONN ALAN PENNEBAKER (JULY 15, 1925 - AUGUST 1, 2019)

ORIGINALLY FROM ILLINOIS, DONN PENNEBAKER TOOK HIS FIRST STEPS AS A DOCUMENTARY FILMMAKER BY SHOOTING *DON'T LOOK BACK* (1967), BOB DYLAN'S UK TOUR OF 1965. HE ATTRACTED IMMEDIATE ATTENTION FOR HIS "DIRECT CINEMA" STYLE AND THE WAY HE CAPTURED LIVE PERFORMANCES AND WAS HIRED TO FILM THE MYTHICAL MONTEREY FESTIVAL OF SUMMER '67, WHICH MADE A STAR OUT OF JANIS JOPLIN. MANY OF HIS SUBSEQUENT FILMS WERE ALSO INTRICATELY LINKED TO THE MUSIC WORLD, WITH SUBJECTS, AMONG OTHERS, LIKE DAVID BOWIE, JIMI HENDRIX, DEPECHE MODE AND JERRY LEE LEWIS.

CLIVE DAVIS (APRIL 4, 1932 -)

BORN IN BROOKLYN, CLIVE DAVIS PRACTICED LAW BEFORE BECOMING A RECORD PRODUCER. SHORTLY AFTER HE BECAME THE PRESIDENT OF CBS RECORDS (PREVIOUSLY COLUMBIA RECORDS), WHICH UP UNTIL THEN HAD NOT FOCUSED MUCH ON ROCK, HE ATTENDED THE MONTEREY FESTIVAL IN THE SUMMER OF '67, WHERE HE DISCOVERED JANIS JOPLIN AND BIG BROTHER AND THE HOLDING COMPANY. HE SIGNED THE BAND A FEW MONTHS LATER. IN ADDITION TO CBS, WHICH HE LEFT IN 1973, CLIVE DAVIS ALSO HEADED UP THE ARISTA AND BMG RECORD LABELS.

JAMES MARSHALL « JIMI » HENDRIX (NOVEMBER 27, 1942 - SEPTEMBER 18, 1970)

BORN IN SEATTLE, JIMI HENDRIX WAS A PRODIGY MUSICIAN WHO FIRST SET THE MUSIC WORLD ON FIRE WITH HIS BREAKTHROUGH PERFORMANCE IN LONDON IN 1966. A SKILLED GUITARIST, HE ONLY HAD TIME TO RECORD FOUR "OFFICIAL" ALBUMS BEFORE HIS ACCIDENTAL DEATH--MOST LIKELY OVERDOSING ON BARBITURATES--BUT HIS POSTHUMOUS DISCOGRAPHY IS CONSIDERABLE. HE WAS RUMORED TO HAVE BRIEFLY BEEN ONE OF JANIS JOPLIN'S MANY LOVERS AND, LIKE JOPLIN, BECAME PART OF THE INFAMOUS 27 CLUB, A GROUP OF MUSICIANS AND ARTISTS IN THEIR ARTISTIC PRIME WHO DIED AT THE PREMATURE AGE OF TWENTY-SEVEN.

JOSEPH ALLEN « COUNTRY JOE » McDONALD (JANUARY 1, 1942 -)

BORN IN WASHINGTON, D.C. AND RAISED IN CALIFORNIA, JOSEPH MCDONALD BEGAN PERFORMING IN THE STREETS OF BERKELEY IN THE EARLY 60S. IN 1965, HE AND HIS MUSICAL PARTNER BARRY "THE FISH" MELTON STARTED THE BAND COUNTRY JOE AND THE FISH. HE RECORDED SEVERAL DOZENS OF ALBUMS THAT WERE MOSTLY ONLY MARGINALLY SUCCESSFUL, YET HE NEVERTHELESS MANAGED TO ACHIEVE NOTORIETY, PRIMARILY FOR TWO REASONS: FOR GETTING THE CROWD AT WOODSTOCK TO SCREAM "FUCK" IN REFERENCE TO THE VIETNAM WAR, AND FOR HAVING BEEN JOPLIN'S "OFFICIAL" FIANCÉ FOR SEVERAL MONTHS- A RECORD FOR A WOMAN THAT RARELY HELD ON TO HER LOVERS FOR MORE THAN A FEW NIGHTS.

ERIC PATRICK CLAPTON (MARCH 30, 1945 -)

BORN IN ENGLAND, ERIC CLAPTON HAS BEEN A LEGENDARY FIGURE OF ROCK FOR DECADES. HE HAS BEEN PERFORMING ON STAGE VIRTUALLY WITHOUT INTERRUPTION SINCE 1963, INCLUDING WITH HIS FIRST PROFESSIONAL BAND, THE YARDBIRDS. HE HAS INFLUENCED SEVERAL GENERATIONS OF MUSICIANS, WHILE CLAIMING THAT HE HIMSELF WAS INSPIRED BY THE GREAT NAMES IN BLUES, THE GENRE THAT CONTINUES TO INFLUENCE HIS MUSIC.

JAMES DOUGLAS « JIM » MORRISON (DECEMBER 8, 1943 - JULY 3, 1971)

JIM MORRISON WAS BORN IN FLORIDA AND GREW UP IN VARIOUS STATES, INCLUDING CALIFORNIA. AS A TEENAGER, HE HAD A MAGNETIC POWER OF ATTRACTION ON ANYONE WHO CAME NEAR HIM. HE ROSE TO METEORIC FAME WITH HIS BAND THE DOORS: SIX ALBUMS IN FIVE YEARS AND INTERNATIONAL STARDOM. THE SINGER DIED IN PARIS IN UNCERTAIN CIRCUMSTANCES (THE OFFICIAL CAUSE OF DEATH WAS A HEART ATTACK, PERHAPS DUE TO AN OVERDOSE) AND WAS LAID TO REST AT THE PÈRE LACHAISE CEMETERY IN PARIS. LIKE JANIS JOPLIN AND JIMI HENDRIX BEFORE HIM, HE WAS 27 YEARS OLD AT THE TIME OF HIS DEATH.

LEONARD COHEN (SEPTEMBER 21, 1934 - NOVEMBER 7, 2016)

LEONARD COHEN WAS A CANADIAN POET AND MUSICIAN (BORN IN THE MONTREAL SUBURB OF WESTMOUNT) AND ONE OF THE GREAT NAMES IN FOLK MUSIC. HIS LYRICS AND SONGS MADE HIM FAMOUS STARTING IN THE 60S ON AND WERE AN INFLUENCE ON MANY ARTISTS. HE IMMORTALIZED HIS ROMANTIC ENCOUNTER WITH JANIS JOPLIN AT NEW YORK CITY'S FAMED CHELSEA HOTEL IN A 1972 SONG, *CHELSEA HOTEL NO. 2.*

JOHN SIMON (AUGUST 11, 1941 -)

BORN IN CONNECTICUT AND RAISED IN A MUSIC-LOVING HOME, JOHN SIMON BEGAN WORKING IN MUSIC PRODUCTION FOR COLUMBIA RECORDS IN THE 1960S. AFTER PRODUCING THE ALBUM *SONGS OF LEONARD COHEN* (1967) AND THE FIRST ALBUM OF BLOOD, SWEAT & TEARS, HE WORKED WITH SIMON AND GARFUNKEL AND THEN JANIS JOPLIN AND BIG BROTHER AND THE HOLDING COMPANY, PRODUCING THEIR CELEBRATED *CHEAP THRILLS* ALBUM. HE ALSO WORKED WITH THE BAND, WHICH TOURED EXTENSIVELY WITH BOB DYLAN UNTIL THE MID-1970S.

ROBERT CRUMB (AUGUST 30, 1943 –)

ONE OF THE GIANTS OF AMERICAN COMICS, ROBERT CRUMB WAS BORN IN PHILADELPHIA AND HAS LIVED IN FRANCE FOR SEVERAL DECADES. HE EMBARKED ON HIS ARTISTIC PATH IN 1962 AND HAS PRODUCED AN IMPRESSIVE BODY OF WORK, INCLUDING OUTSTANDING DEPICTIONS OF LIFE IN CALIFORNIA DURING THE FLOWER POWER ERA, IN THE YEARS WHEN HE WAS LIVING IN SAN FRANCISCO. HIS COVER FOR BIG BROTHER AND THE HOLDING COMPANY'S 1968 *CHEAP THRILLS* ALBUM WAS EXTREMELY INNOVATIVE FOR THE TIMES AND WENT DOWN IN HISTORY.

STANLEY BOOTH (JANUARY 5, 1942 –)

BORN IN GEORGIA, BUT BASED IN MEMPHIS, TENNESSEE, STANLEY BOOTH IS ONE OF THE GREAT NAMES IN THE HISTORY OF MUSICAL JOURNALISM IN THE U.S. HE FIRST MADE A NAME FOR HIMSELF IN THE MID-60'S WITH HIS ATTENTION-GETTING PIECES ON ARTISTS SUCH AS ELVIS PRESLEY AND OTIS REDDING. HIS ARTICLES HAVE BEEN PUBLISHED BY *ESQUIRE, ROLLING STONE* AND *GQ*, AMONG OTHERS. IN 1968, HE WAS IN ATTENDANCE AT THE CONCERT GIVEN BY JANIS JOPLIN IN MEMPHIS AT THE STAX LABEL CHRISTMAS PARTY. HE HAS ALSO WRITTEN EXTENSIVELY ABOUT THE ROLLING STONES, AND IS CONSIDERED ONE OF THEIR MAJOR BIOGRAPHERS.

DICK CAVETT (NOVEMBER 19, 1936 –)

A TV PERSONALITY AND TALK SHOW HOST FROM NEBRASKA, DICK CAVETT HOSTED THE IMMENSELY POPULAR *DICK CAVETT SHOW* IN THE 60S, 70S AND 80S, WHICH INITIALLY AIRED ON ABC BEFORE IT MOVED TO CBS AND LATER TO PBS. COUNTLESS CELEBRITIES FROM THE FILM, SPORTS AND ARTS WORLDS APPEARED ON HIS SHOW OVER THE YEARS, INCLUDING MARLON BRANDO, TRUMAN CAPOTE, MOHAMED ALI, GROUCHO MARX AND ALAIN DELON. JANIS JOPLIN WAS HIS FEATURED GUEST ON SEVERAL OCCASIONS (THE LAST TIME WAS ON AUGUST 3, 1970, EXACTLY TWO MONTHS BEFORE SHE DIED), AND THERE WAS A CHEMISTRY BETWEEN THE TWO THAT WAS HARD NOT TO NOTICE. .

MICHAEL LANG (DECEMBER 11, 1944 –)

BORN IN BROOKLYN, MICHAEL LANG MADE A NAME FOR HIMSELF IN THE SECOND HALF OF THE 1960S AS A PRODUCER AND CONCERT PROMOTER. HE IS BEST KNOWN FOR BEING ONE OF THE MAIN ORGANIZERS OF THE WOODSTOCK FESTIVAL IN AUGUST OF '69, WHERE HE MET JANIS JOPLIN, ONE OF THE EVENT'S HEADLINERS.

SETH DAVID MORGAN (APRIL 4, 1949 – OCTOBER 17, 1990)

ONE OF THE SONS OF NEW YORK POET GEORGE FREDERICK MORGAN AND JANIS JOPLIN'S LAST "OFFICIAL" BOYFRIEND, SETH MORGAN WAS A BOASTFUL MANIPULATOR WHOM MOST OF THE SINGER'S FRIENDS AND ACQUAINTANCES REMEMBERED AS AN UNSAVORY CHARACTER. HE WROTE A NOVEL IN 1990 THAT WAS PUBLISHED SHORTLY BEFORE HE DIED IN A MOTORCYCLE ACCIDENT IN NEW ORLEANS WHILE DRUNK AND HIGH.

KRIS KRISTOFFERSON (JUNE 22, 1936 –)

BORN IN BROWNSVILLE, TEXAS AND RAISED IN CALIFORNIA, KRISS KRISTOFFERSON HAD A DOUBLE CAREER AS A MUSICIAN AND AN ACTOR STARTING IN THE LATE 60S (OVER SIXTY FILMS SINCE THE FIRST ONE IN 1971). IN 1970, HE GAVE JANIS JOPLIN THE GIFT OF ONE OF HIS COMPOSITIONS, *ME AND BOBBY MCGEE*, BEFORE PERFORMING IT HIMSELF LATER THAT SAME YEAR. THE TRACK WENT ON TO BECOME ONE OF THE BIG HITS FROM THE PEARL ALBUM. .

PAUL ALLEN ROTHCHILD (APRIL 18, 1935 - MARCH 30, 1995)

BORN IN BROOKLYN TO A FAMILY OF MUSICIANS, PAUL ROTHCHILD EXPRESSED AN EARLY INTEREST IN MUSIC PRODUCTION AND BEGAN WORKING WITH JAC HOLZMAN'S LABEL ELEKTRA IN THE MID-1960S, PRODUCING AMONG OTHERS THE EARLY ALBUMS OF THE PAUL BUTTERFIELD BLUES BAND. HE MOVED TO LOS ANGELES IN 1965, WHERE HE PRODUCED MANY OF THE GREAT ALBUMS OF THE TIME, BY ARTISTS SUCH AS THE DOORS, JONI MITCHELL, NEIL YOUNG, AND TIM BUCKLEY. HE WAS THE PRODUCER OF JANIS JOPLIN'S LAST ALBUM, *PEARL*.

NICHOLAS GEORGE « NICK » GRAVENITES (OCTOBER 12, 1938 -)

AUTHOR, COMPOSER AND MUSICIAN NICK GRAVENITES WAS BORN IN CHICAGO BUT MOVED TO CALIFORNIA EARLY ON, WHERE HE BECAME ONE OF THE KEY FIGURES IN THE LOCAL MUSIC SCENE IN THE '60S. AFTER A STINT WITH THE PAUL BUTTERFIELD BLUES BAND, HE AND MIKE BLOOMFIELD STARTED THE ELECTRIC FLAG BAND IN 1967, AN ENDEAVOR THAT SEEMED PROMISING AT FIRST BUT NEVER REALLY TOOK OFF. OVER HIS EXTENSIVE MUSICAL CAREER, NICK GRAVENITES HAS APPEARED IN THE CREDITS OF SOME FORTY ALBUMS. HE IS ONE OF THE MAIN CONTRIBUTORS TO JANIS JOPLIN'S PEARL ALBUM, WHOSE *BURIED ALIVE IN THE BLUES* IS HIS COMPOSITION.

MYRA FRIEDMAN (MAY 3, 1932 - OCTOBER 16, 2010)

BORN IN NEW YORK, MYRA FRIEDMAN JOINED ALBERT GROSSMAN'S AGENCY IN EARLY 1968 AS A PUBLICIST, AND IT WAS IN THAT CAPACITY THAT SHE MET JANIS JOPLIN, ONE OF HER MOST FAMOUS CLIENTS. THE TWO WOMEN BECAME GOOD FRIENDS, AND FRIEDMAN DREW FROM HER EXPERIENCE AS THE SIGNER'S CONFIDANT TO PEN A 1973 BIOGRAPHICAL PORTRAIT OF HER TITLED *BURIED ALIVE*.

FURTHER READING AND VIEWING

BOOKS

I Ran Into Some Trouble

by Peggy Caserta Author), Maggie Falcon (Author)

The memoir that follows up an earlier and more scandalous, tell-all memoir by Joplin's friend, drug buddy and lover Peggy Caserta, in which, among other things, the author calls into question a heroin overdose as her friend's cause of death.

"A chronicle of Caserta's life before, with and after Joplin, *I Ran into Some Trouble* is a riveting cautionary tale of the wild ride and dark side of the counterculture." -- *Rolling Stone*

Buried Alive: The Biography of Janis Joplin

By Myra Friedman

An intimate portrayal of the star from her friend and publicist.

"One of the best books about a rock figure thus far...Buried Alive is unquestionably an accomplishment and it may well be the best portrait we'll have of Janis!" -- *Rolling Stone*

"Brilliant, marvelous, emotionally devastating...I don't think there's anything about Janis the book leaves untouched....I can almost hear her speak and, more relevantly, hear her laugh." -- *New York Daily News*

Janis - Her Life and Music

By Holly George-Warren

"This gripping biography charts the brilliant and troubled blues singer, from life in small-town Texas to discovering Kerouac, San Francisco, and her own musical self." – *Vanity Fair*

"....[tells] her story simply and well, with some of the tone and flavor of a good novel." – *The New York Times*

FILMS

The Life and Music of Janis Joplin (1974).

Directed by Howard Alk; documentary about Joplin's life from Texas to fame, featuring interviews and concert footage of her and Big Brother and the Holding Company.

The Rose (1979)

Directed by Mark Rydell and starring Bette Middler as a self-destructive rock star who struggles with addiction and the pressures of fame, and loosely based on the life of Janis Joplin. Nominated for four Academy Awards, including best actress. Middler performed the soundtrack and the title track became one of her biggest singles.

Janis: Little Girl Blue (2015.)

Documentary directed by Amy Berg. Musician Cat Power narrates this documentary on Janis Joplin's rise to fame from letters that Joplin wrote over the years to her friends, family, and collaborators.

YOUTUBE

Find her acclaimed appearances on the Dick Cavett show; a documentary that reconstructs the last 24 hours of her life; recordings; concert footage from Woodstock, the Monterey Pop Festival of 1967, and other events; a 1968 lost backstage radio interview with the acclaimed oral historian of American lives, Studs Terkel, put to video with accompanying gorgeous black and white photos; and much more.

WEBSITES

Both WWW.JANISJOPLIN.NET and WWW.JANISJOPLIN.com feature all sorts of biographical information, books, albums, articles, interviews, news, and more.

ARTICLES

There have obviously been countless articles about Joplin over the years. Of special interest with reference to a passage in this graphic novel, is "How Leonard Cohen Met Janis Joplin: Inside the Legendary Chelsea Hotel Encounter," by Jordan Runtagh, for *Rolling Stone*, in which Cohen tells of the encounter in his own words and the author waxes poetic on the famed Chelsea Hotel and its bohemian clientele.